TAKE NO PRISONERS

TAKE NO PRISONERS

THE BATTLE PLAN FOR DEFEATING THE LEFT

DAVID HOROWITZ

REGNERY
PUBLISHING

A Salem Communications Company

Library of Congress Control Number 2014941644

ISBN 978-1-62157-256-5

Published in the United States by
Regnery Publishing
A Salem Communications Company
300 New Jersey Ave NW
Washington, DC 20001
www.Regnery.com

Distributed to the trade by
Perseus Distribution
250 West 57th Street
New York, NY 10107

Manufactured in the United States of America

10 9 8 7 6 5 4 3 2 1

Books are available in quantity for promotional or premium use. For information on discounts and terms, please visit our website: www.Regnery.com.

*Special thanks to Jerry and Marilyn Hayden
for helping to make this book possible.*

CONTENTS

INTRODUCTION: Happy Warriors..xi

PART ONE

CHAPTER 1 Go for the Heart 1

CHAPTER 2 Defend Our Country 23

CHAPTER 3 The Progressive Threat 39

CHAPTER 4 Fight Fire with Fire... 55

CHAPTER 5 Uniting the Right 69

CHAPTER 6 Destructive Social Justice 79

CHAPTER 7 The Tea Party and the GOP:
Can This Marriage Survive? 107

PART TWO

CHAPTER 8 The Art of Political War.. 117

CHAPTER 9 How to Beat the Democrats 139

ACKNOWLEDGMENTS 165

NOTES 167

INDEX 193

Everyone has a game plan until you punch them in the mouth.
—CHRIS LEHANE,
DEMOCRATIC STRATEGIST

INTRODUCTION

HAPPY WARRIORS

It doesn't take an expert to notice that Republicans have been pursuing a failed political strategy and win elections only when Democrats screw up big time. The Democrats' electoral victories are not explained by the success of their signature programs. Social Security, the War on Poverty, and Medicare are all either bankrupt or, in the case of the War on Poverty, an abject failure. Under Democratic policies of the last fifty years, the federal government has spent more than $20 trillion to eliminate poverty.[1] Yet today more Americans are officially "poor" than when Lyndon Johnson squandered the first taxpayer dollar.[2] Worse, the beneficiaries of Democrat welfare programs have become a permanently dependent class with little chance of improving their lot. How is it possible that although Democrat policies have caused so much misery and failed so dramatically, Democrat candidates have won the popular vote in five of the last six presidential elections? The answer lies in their superior political strategy. This book analyzes why it is superior and explains how Republicans can turn it to their own advantage and win.

One of the obstacles to Republican success is the pessimism that seems to be carried as a conservative gene. Every year, I host a conference for conservatives called the Restoration Weekend.[3] The idea for the event was lifted from Democrats who began holding "Renaissance Weekends" during the Clinton administration. "Renaissance" means "rebirth." A good way to think about Democrats is that they don't regard the past as experience to be learned from but as dead wood to be discarded. Progressives believe that with enough power and enough money, they can create a new—and immeasurably better—world than the one we know. With enough prompting from the state, the rest of us can be refashioned into a species whose members get along naturally and share their earnings with strangers. Eventually each will give according to his ability and receive according to his need. Everyone will have enough, and everyone will be taken care of.[4]

In other words, progressives haven't figured out what the human tragedies of the twentieth century should have taught them: socialism doesn't work. Human beings are not designed to fit their progressive paradise. Consequently, progressives' benevolent schemes require government coercion at every level—Obamacare mandates are just the beginning—to force the reluctant and ornery to comply. And even then they will not work. The miseries created by socialist experiments should have demonstrated once and for all that "social justice" is a fantasy beyond the reach of mere mortals. It requires a transformation that only a divine intervention could pull off. When human beings attempt it themselves, the results can be catastrophic, and the messes bigger than any they set out to fix.

The name "Restoration Weekend" came to me during the Clinton years because progressives were in the White House and it was a cute way of proposing an opposition agenda. But I soon realized that the name was fitting for another reason. It relates to the perennial gloom that hovers like a cloud over the conservative mind, encouraging a fatalism that can prove politically deadly. In politics, as in any conflict, if you think you are going to lose, you probably will. Indeed, if you are a pessimist by nature, you probably shouldn't be in politics in the first place. If you believe—as former presidential nominee Mitt Romney and an alarming number of his supporters did—that 47 percent of the electorate can't be persuaded to vote for a conservative, because they get "stuff" from the government, you shouldn't be in politics. After all, every four years Democrats seem able to sell snake oil pretty well. Politics is the art of turning voters' heads. If people simply voted with their pocket books, nobody with a taxable income would vote for a Democrat. But an awful lot of them do. If you think voters are too "low information" to be persuaded, you probably shouldn't be in politics either. Politics is about winning hearts and minds. On the field of battle, armies have often won despite unpromising odds. If you are not up to this task, leave it to those who are.

In November 2013, Restoration Weekend featured Senator Ted Cruz and Dr. Ben Carson as keynote speakers. This particular November was when the $600 million Obamacare website was crashing on launch. It was a month when the president's lies about Obamacare were being exposed, his approval ratings were dropping to record lows, and his signal achievement was imploding.[5] It was a month when Democrats were panicking at the prospect of a Republican tsunami in the congressional elections only a year away. Yet conservatives coming to the Weekend were depressed. One after another voiced anxiety about the political future. "Do you see how big the deficit has become and how fast the debt is growing?" "Can you believe the dishonesty of this president, how he has encouraged our enemies and betrayed our friends and brought our nation low?" "How can we possibly stop this nightmare when there are all those low-information voters ready to believe what the Democrats say? Even if we could persuade them, Republicans will probably screw up the elections and return the culprits to power."

This book is my answer to such conservative worries and doubts. To begin with, it's not conservative to blame others for the plight in which you find yourself. In politics, as in other battles, what is decisive is how you fight. If you are losing, you need to look to yourself for the reason why you are not doing better. It is the only way to improve the situation. Take responsibility, both personal and collective, for what has happened. That's a conservative idea. Another is to show respect for the American Founding. The men who created this republic made its people sovereign. Our democracy is built on the belief that, given the chance, the American people in the long run will do the right thing. If conservatives want to win, they need to embrace this faith.

The strategy outlined in these pages contains the working principles of a political messaging and consulting group I have formed called Take No Prisoners Campaigns. Information on this organization is available at www.TakeNoPrisonersCampaigns.org.

PART ONE

CHAPTER ONE

GO FOR THE HEART

After voters went to the polls in November 2012 and reelected a president who had increased the nation's debt by $5 trillion, left 23 million Americans unemployed, abandoned Iraq to America's enemy Iran, and abetted the Muslim Brotherhood in its bid to control the most important country in the Middle East, the one conclusion Republicans should have been able to draw is that elections are driven by emotions, not reason. And when it comes to mobilizing political emotions, Democrats beat Republicans, hands down.

Republicans have lost the popular vote in five of the last six presidential elections, yet they seem unable to learn basic facts from their losses. Year after year and election after election, the Democrats' campaign themes are monotonously the same. They scare voters by accusing Republicans of imaginary crimes. And always the same crimes: Republicans wage wars on women, on minorities, and on the vulnerable. They defend the rich and don't care about the poor. Their policies inflict pain on working families to benefit the wealthy few. Year after year, the Democrats repeat these attacks, and year after year, Republicans fail to come up with effective responses. Worse, they don't present voters with answers that neutralize the attacks, or take the battle to the enemy camp.

The 2012 presidential election presented a model of this impasse. Second-term elections are usually referendums on the incumbent's record. Democrats were running a wounded incumbent who could not reasonably run on his performance in office. Virtually every commentator predicted the Democrats would be forced to rely on a negative campaign to damage their opponent enough to defeat him, which they did.[1] By July, the *National Journal* was reporting that Obama's "campaign has taken an overwhelmingly negative turn at a time when the economic recovery is stalling, and it buttresses what the Republicans have been saying for months: The president's overall strategy is to ruin Romney's reputation, leaving voters without a viable alternative."[2] The Obama ads portrayed Romney as a defender of the "1 percent" who were not paying their "fair share," an abuser of the family dog, and a corporate predator who just didn't care. The Romney-Republican response to these attacks was to deplore them as "class warfare rhetoric" and "divisive."

These were weak and whiny responses, all too familiar from previous Republican campaigns. Common to both was the failure to address the specific charges. They did not answer the claim that Republicans defended the wealthy and didn't care about the rest. There were plenty of answers to these libels, but Republicans didn't have them. They certainly didn't have responses that would put Democrats—instead of themselves—on the defensive. This could only be accomplished by an attack on the Democrats as the party that didn't care.

At election time, "caring" is not one issue among many. It is the central one. Most issues are complex and require more information than the public can readily acquire. Consequently, voters care less about policy details than about the candidates who are going to shape them. Voters don't get to decide the policies. They elect their representatives to do that for them. They want to know whom they can rely on to sort out the complexities and vote in their best interests. Above everything else, they want to know whom they can trust to make those decisions. They want to know who cares about *them*. Although for some voters a policy position can be decisive, for most—and particularly for the "undecideds"—far more important is a candidate who cares about them.

How crucial is their desire for a candidate who cares? In the 2012 election, 70 percent of Asian Americans cast their ballots for Barack Obama even though he did not share their values or produce the economic recovery he had promised—or even pay much attention to them as a group. The vast majority of Asian Americans voted for the Democrat even though they hold Republican values. Asian Americans are family oriented, entrepreneurial, and traditional. They voted for Obama because they believed he cared for minorities—for *them*—and the Republican Romney didn't.

The Republican response to Democrats' attacks is ineffective because it speaks to voters in a language that is abstract, unemotional, and indirect. "Divisive politics" and "class warfare rhetoric" are phrases that lack a human face. They have no emotional appeal. "Class warfare rhetoric" is the description of a political style. There are certainly critics of political style among the voting public, but they do not decide elections. The Democratic attack, by contrast, is a direct hit on an easily identified human target: the wealthy few. The Democratic attack appeals to the base emotions of envy, resentment, and fear. An electoral attack should always sting, and an attack like this does. It does more. It tells voters who are not rich that somebody cares about *them*.

Using the term "class warfare" is a polite way of discussing a real problem, namely leftist agendas in national politics. But politeness protects others—in this case, opponents who are busy defaming you as mean spirited and selfish. A term like "class warfare" sounds ideological—not an asset in a general election. More important, it fails to hold your adversaries accountable for what they have actually done and are likely to continue doing if elected. The complaint about "class warfare rhetoric" doesn't give voters a reason to vote for you and not them. Complaining about "divisive politics" is not only futile, it is incomprehensible. Elections are by nature divisive. They are competitions between winners and losers. They are about defeating opponents. Why *wouldn't* they be divisive?

Because elections are divisive, they are about "us" and "them." Electoral campaigns should be about why we are your friends and advocates, and they are not. Defining your opponent is the first order of business of any political campaign. Democrats are skilled professionals at this negative side of the campaign business, and Republicans are inept amateurs. Democrats know how to frame an indictment, how to incite envy and resentment, how to inspire fear and distrust. And they know how to direct inflammatory emotions against their Republican targets. Meanwhile, Republicans are complaining about the style of the Democrats' *arguments* when they should be attacking Democrats for who they are and what they have done to the voting public they claim to serve. Here is a sound bite from the familiar political debate:

> DEMOCRATS: The Republicans are defending the rich at your expense.

> REPUBLICANS: The Democrats are using class warfare rhetoric.

Which argument is going to grab voters? Which is going to make voters believe the candidate cares about *them*? The answer couldn't be more obvious. This is why, despite the bankrupt policies they have inflicted on the country and are proposing to inflict again, Democrats win elections against their Republican opponents.

On the day of the 2012 presidential election, a CNN exit poll asked, "What is the most important candidate quality to your vote?" and offered respondents a choice of answers that included (1) Strong leader, (2) Shares your values, (3) Has a vision for the future, and (4) Cares about people. Romney won the votes of 54 percent or more of the people who selected one of the first three answers. In other words, he represented the values and vision the voters wanted and would have won the election if it had been decided by those factors alone. But Romney lost "cares about people" voters by 81 to 18 percent. That drubbing tells you everything you need to know about why Republicans lose elections.[3]

The margin by which Romney lost the presidential election wasn't insurmountable. He had the advantage of running in a good Republican year. People were smarting from the slowest economic recovery in memory. They didn't like Obama's signature legislation, the Affordable Care Act. In the midterm elections of 2010, they had voted Democrats out of office in record numbers, largely over this issue. Coming into the 2012 presidential election, Republican voters were intense. Every activist on the Right thought that the fate of the country hung in the balance. By contrast, Democrats went into the campaign with a substantial segment of their political base disappointed by their performance. They had failed to produce a job recovery and were presiding over an economy with high unemployment among their key constituencies—women, Hispanics, and African Americans—all victims of Democrat policies, though you wouldn't know it from listening to the Romney campaign. They had kept open a prison in Guantanamo they had promised to close and had continued wars they had promised to terminate. Yet the Democrats were still able to arouse enough fear and anger to energize their base and win.

Behind Republican failures at the ballot box is an attitude that reflects an administrative rather than political approach to election campaigns. Republicans focus on policy proposals rather than on electoral combat and the threat posed by their opponents. Administrative politicians are more comfortable with budgets and pie charts than with the flesh-and-blood victims of their opponents' policies and ideas. When Republicans do appeal to the victims of the Democrats' policies, those victims are frequently small business owners and other job creators—people who in the eyes of most Americans are rich.

To the accusation that they are defenders of the comfortable and afflicters of the weak, Republicans really have only one answer; and that answer sounds like a complaint: "That's divisive. It's class warfare." Even if most voters were able to access the relevant facts (and for many reasons they are not), the complaint itself requires explaining to make any sense. But discursive appeals to reason are quickly buried in the raucous noise of the electoral battlefield. Sorting out the truth would be a daunting task even if voters were left alone to make up their minds. But they are not left alone. They are assaulted by thousands of TV and electronic messages that overwhelm them with contradictory data and malicious distortions. These deceptions are not inadvertent. They are the deliberate work of the professionals who run political campaigns—and these campaigns hire them *because* they are experts in disinformation and misrepresentation. In the world outside politics, this is called lying; in politics, it's called *spin*, and to one extent or another everybody does it. But Democrats do it far better and far more aggressively than their Republican targets. Democrats' lies are aimed at Republican *character*. They are up close and personal and not at all abstract.

DEMOCRATS ARE DIFFERENT

There is a reason for this difference in tactics, and it affects everything that goes on in political campaigns. Republicans and Democrats are not simply people who make opposing judgments about the solutions to common problems—for example, that spending is good or tax hikes are bad. Republicans and Democrats approach politics with fundamentally different visions of what politics is about. These visions color not only the way each side thinks about questions of policy, but how they face their opponents in the arena.

The Democratic Party is no longer the party of John F. Kennedy, whose politics were identical to Ronald Reagan's (militant anti-Communist, military hawk, in favor of a capital gains tax cut and a balanced budget). It is not even the party of Hubert Humphrey, who supported the Vietnam War, a conflict that every contemporary Democratic legislator and operative opposes in retrospect, and that many, like John Kerry and Bill and Hillary Clinton, opposed at the time. The Democratic Party has moved steadily leftward since the 1972 presidential campaign of George McGovern until it is now a party of the Left, led by progressives who are convinced that their policies are way stations on the path to a "better world."

The vision of moral and social progress that Democrats share has profound consequences for the way they conduct their political battles. Unlike conservatives, progressives are not in politics merely to improve government practices and ameliorate social problems. They are missionaries who want to "change society" and "solve" its problems. They are out to create an entirely new order, which they call "social justice." They think of themselves as social redeemers. Their belief in a redeemed future accounts for their political passion and for their furious personal assaults on those who stand in their way.

In 1996, Senator Bob Dole—a moderate Republican dealmaker—ran for president against the incumbent, Bill Clinton, a centrist Democrat. At the time, Dick Morris was Clinton's political advisor. As they were heading into the election campaign, Clinton told Morris, "You have to understand, Dick, Bob Dole is evil."[4] That is how even moderate Democrats like Clinton view the political battle. Republicans see Democrats as mistaken. Democrats see Republicans as enemies of the just and the good. There is no parallel Republican belief that drives their emotions and agendas.

If Democrats' priority were fixing government problems, would they have failed to produce a budget for four straight years, as they did during Obama's first term, in the midst of a financial crisis? If Democrats were pragmatists, wouldn't they have immediately sought a bipartisan approach to the crisis that confronted them when they took office in January 2009? This is exactly what Obama promised he would do during the campaign, and it's one of the reasons he was elected. But it is the opposite of what he did when he entered the Oval Office and launched the most divisive legislation—Obamacare—since the Civil War. Instead of focusing on jobs and the economy, he spent his first two years pushing a massive new entitlement program. If Obama and the Democrats were concerned about dealing with the jobs crisis, they would not have used their monopoly of power to pursue a new trillion-dollar social program opposed by half the nation and by *every* Republican in Congress. But they were not as interested in addressing the crisis as they were in using it as leverage to launch their society-transforming schemes.[5]

The Democrats made Obamacare their priority because they are social missionaries whose goal is to "fundamentally transform" the United States of America, as Obama warned five days before the 2008 election. Creating a massive new government program that would absorb one-sixth of the economy and make every American dependent on government for his health needs was the first item on the Democrats' missionary agenda. They saw it as a milestone on the way to a brave new future. That is the way progressives think, and their opponents had better understand what that means. Progressives are not in politics to tinker with the existing system, although they understand that tinkering and fixing problems along the way will gain them votes. They are in politics to transform the way Americans live.

Why do progressives not see that the future they are promoting has already failed elsewhere? First, because they see history as something to transcend, not as providing a reservoir of experience from which they must learn. Second, because in their eyes the future is an idea that has not yet been tried. If socialism failed in Europe, it's because *they* weren't the ones implementing it, and the conditions weren't right to make it work.

The very grandeur of their ambition turns progressives into zealots. They dream of using the power of the state to make everyone equal and to take care of everyone's needs. They are going to legislate—and dictate— social equality and social justice. How intoxicating is that idea? It explains why progressives approach politics differently from conservatives. It doesn't matter to progressives that the massive entitlement programs they created—Social Security and Medicare—are already bankrupt. They can take care of that by making wealthy people pay their "fair share." Progressives believe that if they can appropriate enough money and accumulate enough power, they can make their glorious future work. Everything Democrats do and every campaign they conduct is about mobilizing their political resources to bring about this result. It is about social transformation—one program and one candidate at a time. No Republican in his right mind thinks like this.

Of course, progressives also seek the power and perks of office for their own sake. What makes them different from other politicians is not these petty ambitions, but the grand mission. The vision of a noble future that they will bring about salves their consciences and puts urgency into their crusades while encouraging their destructive attacks. A Republican like Mitt Romney may be a decent person, but because he stands in the way of their noble dreams, he may be regarded as "evil." The nobility of the progressive vision—comprehensive healthcare, housing and food for everyone, equality for all, a planet saved—inspires them to seek the promised land by any means available. If the end requires lying, voter fraud, and demonizing their opponents as racist, selfish, and uncaring, so be it. The beautiful goal justifies the ugly means.

When Democrats demand government subsidies for contraceptives and then scream that Republican opponents are waging a war on women, Republicans shake their heads in disbelief. How could any sane person believe that? But Republicans are missing the point. For progressives, the issue is never the issue. The issue is always the social transformation in their heads. As Sandra Fluke, the Democrats' contraceptive poster child, put it, the imperative of free contraception is not just about contraception but about the liberation of women, which Republicans oppose.[6] In their view, the more government provides for women (or anyone else), the freer they become. Republicans beg to differ: the more government provides, the more dependent they become.

Progressives' hatred for conservatives is not inspired by a particular issue or a misunderstood remark, as many Republicans like to think. They hate conservatives for what they are: obstructers of the progressive dream. Conservatives believe in individual freedom and limited government. This prescription, by its very nature, spells death for progressive schemes. In other words, as progressives view the world, conservatives and Republicans actually *are* anti-woman, anti-minority, and anti-poor. Republicans stand in the way of the progressive future, which is their liberation. Republicans oppose the very idea that government should function as a social savior. Republicans are reactionary and hateful because they oppose the future in which everyone will be cared for from cradle to grave.

Republicans do not hope to change the world. They are too mindful of the human catastrophes that have been brought about by those who do. Republicans are practical minded. They want to repair policies and procedures that are broken. They are not missionaries, and they are not selling a land of dreams. Their practical agenda makes them regard their opponents not as evil but only in error. It is natural for Republicans to mistake Democrats for dissenting versions of themselves. They think people on the Left do not understand how things work or how to fix them when they are broken. Republicans would like to ameliorate social problems; they do not delude themselves into thinking they could end them for good. Because Republicans are mindful that the past is a cautionary tale, they are uncertain about the future and the consequences of human actions. They are wary of impossible dreams. They understand that many problems are intractable and will not go away. They hope for a future somewhat better than the present but are mindful that things could be made even worse. Much worse.

As a result of this attitude, conservatives' emotions are not inflamed as progressives' are when confronting those with whom they disagree. The conservative instinct is to search for common ground and to arrive at practical measures to address particular problems. That is why they spend a lot of time explaining to voters how their proposals might work. But by the time they reach them, many voters are not listening, because they have been warned not to trust the arguments of enemies of women, children, minorities, and the poor.

This is the emotional hate campaign that Democrats wage in every election. There is only one way to confront and neutralize such attacks. That is through an equally emotional campaign that puts the aggressors on the defensive and indicts them in the same moral language, identifying them as the oppressors of women, children, minorities, and the poor. An attack like this would take away their high ground and put them on the defensive.

TACTICAL PRINCIPLES

1. Put the aggressors on defense.
2. Throw their victims in their faces.
3. Start the campaign now (because they already have).

The weapons of political campaigns are images and sound bites designed to inspire hope and fear. Obama won the presidency in 2008 on a campaign of hope; he won reelection in 2012 on a campaign of fear.

Hope works, but fear is a stronger and more compelling emotion. Democrats stoke voters' fears at every turn, while Republicans often are too polite to do the same. Democrats have a natural advantage in both cases. Their hopes are higher and therefore their fears are more extreme. Republicans are comfortable saying, "It's morning in America." They're not so comfortable saying, "Elect me, and I will make it morning in America." That's a Democrat's campaign promise. Hope is at odds with conservatives' skepticism about the ability of politics to "solve" our human problems. Democrats talk about saving the planet and "repairing the world." Unlike progressives, conservatives don't expect cosmic results from political programs. They don't think of their candidates as "messiahs" the way many otherwise sober Democrats talked about Barack Obama in 2008.[7]

When they do try to offer hope, Republicans do so by proposing very specific solutions to pressing problems. A perfect example is Paul Ryan's plan to balance the federal budget—the "Roadmap for America's Future"—which he first proposed in 2008 and modified in 2010. Paul Ryan is a smart conservative and his plan is probably a good one. Yet who but a policy wonk would know if it were? Since Republicans at the time controlled only the House of Representatives, they had no chance of enacting Ryan's plan into law. So there was not going to be an empirical test of its results. The plan was complicated, and for most voters its details so obscure as to be invisible. Only those voters who trusted the plan's designers would regard it as a reason to vote for the Republican ticket when Ryan was Mitt Romney's running mate in 2012. Republicans passed the "Roadmap" in the House of Representatives, but it was an empty gesture. It was also a politically danger- ous one since it created a target for the opposition. Democrat sharpshoot- ers were given multiple features to aim at and distort. Meanwhile, voters' attention was shifted away from the failing policies of the Democrats to the potential problems of the Ryan plan. As good as it may have been, the plan was both an idle threat and a self-inflicted wound.

Selling hope in politics is an appeal to emotion rather than reason and normally involves large quantities of hot air. It is most effective when pack- aged not as a practical plan but a vague and uplifting promise. In the 2008 election, the hope was embodied in the Democratic candidate who was the first African American with a real chance to become president. The candi- date himself inflated this hope with a multitude of empty promises: "There is not a liberal America and a conservative America; there's the United States of America. There is not a black America and white America and Latino America and Asian America; there's the United States of America."[8] All Obama had to do to inspire hope was to be African American and make gestures—dishonest and empty as they turned out to be—toward uniting Americans and moving the country past its racial and political divisions.

THE CAMPAIGN NARRATIVE

The two emotions that drive politics—hope and fear—are connected through a narrative that runs through all American political contests: the story of the underdog and his triumph over adversity. Both Democrats and Republicans make use of this story, but they do so in dramatically different ways.

For Republicans, it is a story of individuals rising from humble origins because of the opportunities America offers. This was the principal theme of the Republican national convention in 2012, with keynote speeches by Ann Romney, Chris Christie, Marco Rubio, Susana Martinez, and Condoleezza Rice. It was an appeal to voters to protect the values and institutions that made those opportunities possible. It is a good story of hope and was extremely effective in the hands of speakers like Rice. But as a positive story with a heartwarming outcome, it failed to promote the other political emotion—fear—or to direct that fear toward political opponents. Insofar as there was any bite to the Republican narratives, it was drawing attention to policies that block opportunity. Higher taxes and overregulation—too much government—stifle opportunity for Americans who are on the way up. But these obstacles were generally left faceless in the Republican presentations. Consequently, Obama was able to dismiss the Republican argument in his acceptance speech at the Democrats' convention: "All [Republicans] have to offer is the same prescription they've had for the last thirty years: Have a surplus? Try a tax cut. Deficit too high? Try another. Feel a cold coming on? Take two tax cuts, roll back some regulations, and call us in the morning!"[9]

The big problem with the Republican narrative is that it is largely abstract and can be rebutted by abstractions. The Republican narrative is about policies and prescriptions over which reasonable people can disagree: How much opportunity will a 3 or 4 percent tax hike actually stifle? The entire argument remains intellectual until Democrats take it up, and then it becomes emotional. Democrats present themselves as champions of the helpless and the vulnerable. They counter the Republican case by arguing that the private sector doesn't provide *enough* opportunity for those left behind, and government programs are necessary to close the gap. Government intervention is necessary to *provide* opportunity for those who lack it—whatever the tax rate. At the end of the argument, Democrats want to help people who need help. That is a powerful emotional appeal to *all* Americans, including Republicans. If you have enough yourself, you want to help others. The Republican argument looks selfish by contrast: Republicans are mainly for helping *themselves* (don't raise taxes on the rich) or for helping people who can already help themselves. Republicans seem to care most about people who are already able to take advantage of opportunities without government help. Unless you understand how the economic system actually works—how freeing up investment is the key to providing for others—that's a tough position to sympathize with.

By contrast, when Democrats tell *their* underdog story, it is not an abstraction that requires thought and understanding, but a powerful, polarizing, emotionally charged attack. In the Democrat narrative, Republicans are oppressors blocking the underdogs' progress. Republicans are the enemies of hope—in particular, the hopes of society's vulnerable and powerless. It's easy to put faces on these victims. In sum, while Republicans set their narrative in a land of peace, Democrats place theirs on the front lines of a *war*.

Here is a Reuters dispatch from the Democratic convention in Charlotte in September 2012:

> Two dozen Democratic women from the U.S. House of Representatives brought the charge that Republicans are waging a "war on women" to the party's convention stage on Tuesday with sharp denunciations of Republicans on healthcare, equal pay and domestic violence. Led by Nancy Pelosi of California, the only woman to serve as speaker of the U.S. House, the women pressed the party's argument that the Democrats will protect women's interests against what they described as Republican attacks.[10]

The purpose of this spectacle was to establish the campaign's central narrative: Republicans are waging "wars" on women, minorities, and the middle class. The Democrats focused on victim groups they claimed were oppressed—or in the case of minorities, suppressed—by malignant Republicans seeking to turn back the historical clock. Absurd as it may have been, this was a powerful emotional message to voters unarmed with the facts.

There is nothing new about this Democratic strategy. In 1996, a major keynote to the Democratic convention contained this gem: "We need to work as we have never done before between now and November 5th to take the Congress back from…the Republicans, because ladies and gentlemen, brothers and sisters, the Republicans are the real threat. They are the real threat to our women. They are the real threat to our children. They are the real threat to clean water, clean air, and the rich landscape of America."[11]

Republicans are the enemies of women, children, *and* the environment. The man pronouncing this anathema was not a fringe character but the governor of New York and a former presidential prospect, Mario Cuomo. Republicans have been the target of this kind of extremist attack through at least four presidential elections, yet they haven't begun to develop an answer to it, let alone respond in kind. To this day, no Republican speaks like that about Democrats—certainly no Republican who is a national figure and party leader.

The 2012 Democratic convention was not about abstract ideas like the Republicans' opportunity society. It was all about the alleged *victims* of Republicans. It was about how Republicans were the enemies of women, children, minorities, and working Americans. Democrats had been in power for four years, controlling all three branches of government for two of them. But at the 2012 Republican convention, there was almost no litany of the victims of Democrat policies.

In a 2012 election postmortem, Romney's deputy campaign manager analyzed the defeat this way: "The bottom line is that the Obama campaign [had] a candidate that was very hard to lay a glove on because he was somebody that the American people, by and large, had decided that they just liked."[12] This is classic excuse making. Campaigns are supposed to make the other candidate unlikeable, which should not have been difficult, given Obama's deceitful character and many failures in office. The Obama campaign devoted itself to doing just that to the Republican. Several hundred million dollars fueled a barrage of TV ads whose sole purpose was to defame a decent, hardworking, successful American as an untrustworthy predator. The Democrats' effort succeeded in making Romney look bad to a majority of voters.[13] Yet the Romney camp mounted no such negative advertising campaign against Barack Obama in response. Romney even described Obama as "a good man," insulating him from responsibility for his failed policies and unscrupulous attacks. That was the reason Obama was still liked despite the hardships his policies had inflicted on Americans.

Obama's campaign manager attended the same postmortem. His team did not think that their candidate was so likeable that Romney couldn't lay a glove on him. Quite the opposite. The Obama camp's view was that "they would lose the election if it was a referendum on the president."[14] Their campaign strategy was to divert attention from the failings of their own candidate by attacking Romney as an uncaring plutocrat who fired people mercilessly, shipped jobs overseas, was too rich to be concerned about other people, and mistreated his dog.[15]

TAKING A CUE FROM THE DEMOCRATS' WAR PLANS

The Republican campaign featured numerous defenses of "job creators," whom Democrats quickly redefined as rich people who don't pay their fair share. That's the problem with playing a "prevent defense." Most Americans see job creators—employers—as rich people (and if they don't already, Democrats will make sure they do). If you are continually defending the top dogs, you are losing. If you want to change that impression and fight for the underdogs, you must go on the attack: What about the Democrat job *destroyers*? Democrats are *killing* the jobs of working Americans. They are not just "failing to create them," as Republicans would put it.

"Failing to create them" is an antiseptic phrase that makes the Democrats guilty of sins of omission rather than commission. But then, Republicans prefer to soften their blows.

Democrats understand the dynamics of political combat. They targeted Romney with a $200 million ad campaign that depicted him as the nation's number-one job destroyer, the bane of honest, hardworking Americans.[16] "Job destroyer" was a description ill suited to a man whose business was reviving bankrupt companies. But it was—or should have been—a perfect fit for his Democratic opponent. How many jobs did America lose under Obama's anti-business reign? How many African Americans, Latinos, and women did Obama leave unemployed? After four years of Obama and his stimulus measures, the *official* unemployment rate in Detroit, a city Democrats have ruled for fifty years, was 19 percent. Actually, 45 percent of Detroiters—mainly African Americans—were unemployed or no longer looking for work.[17] Thirty-five percent of Detroit's population is on food stamps.[18] What possible conclusion could there be but that Democrats destroy jobs and make people poor, especially blacks and Hispanics in America's Democrat-controlled inner cities? Why wasn't there a $200 million Republican ad campaign with this message?

Why are Republicans so reluctant to name the victims of Democrat policies, particularly the victims among America's minorities and working classes? Why don't Republicans identify Democrats as a *threat* to those people, as Cuomo declared Republicans a threat to women and children? *How can you win a war when the other side is using bazookas and your side is wielding fly swatters?*

Defending the minorities and working Americans who are the victims of the job-destroying Democrats packs an emotional punch that defending rich job creators does not. Defending the victims is morally appealing. It arouses sympathy and anger. It is the only way Republicans can neutralize the Democrats' attacks on them as defenders of the well-to-do and defilers of the helpless. It is the way to return their fire.

As a result of the collapse of the housing market, African Americans—
middle-class African Americans—lost one-half of their net worth.[19] That's
more than a hundred billion dollars in personal assets that disappeared from
the pockets of African Americans. This disaster was the direct result of a
twenty-five-year Democratic campaign—led by Obama and Clinton—to
force banks to write mortgages for people who couldn't afford to pay them.[20]
Yet during the entire 2012 presidential campaign, Republicans were too
polite to mention this.

The campaign to remove standard loan requirements for African
Americans and other minority borrowers began with Jimmy Carter's
Community Reinvestment Act.[21] The removal of these loan requirements
seduced tens of thousands of poor black and Hispanic Americans into
buying homes they couldn't afford, which they then lost. How traumatic
is losing one's home! By securitizing those unsound mortgages, Democratic bundlers on Wall Street made tens of millions off the misery of the
vulnerable and helped to trigger the financial meltdown of 2008. With
the help of the Democrats, Wall Street millionaires made massive profits
off the backs of poor black and Hispanic Americans. Here was a missed
opportunity to neutralize the Democratic slander that Republicans are
the party of the rich and exploiters of the poor. It was an opportunity to
drive a giant wedge through the Democratic base. But it was an opportunity lost.

If Republicans want to persuade minorities they care, they have to stand
up for them. They have to defend them. They have to show that Democrats
are playing them for suckers, that Democrats are exploiting them, oppressing them, and profiting from their suffering. An easy case to make, if there
were Republicans willing to make it.

Large populations of the African American and Hispanic poor are
concentrated in America's inner cities—among them Detroit, Chicago,
Philadelphia, St. Louis, Harlem, and South-Central Los Angeles. In America's inner cities, the unemployment rates are off the charts. The school

systems are so corrupt and ineffective that almost half the children drop out before they graduate, and half those who do graduate are functionally illiterate. They will never get a decent job or a shot at the American dream.

In the middle of the 2012 campaign, a teacher's union strike shut down the schools in Chicago, Obama's hometown. The issue was not salaries but the union's opposition to evaluating teacher performance. Across the nation, in school systems like Chicago's, public school teachers get lifetime tenure after a year or two on the job, guaranteed raises merely for showing up, and job security that makes it impossible to fire them for incompetence. The true victims of this union-enforced and Democrat-backed system are mainly poor African American and Hispanic children whose parents can't afford to buy the private education that most union officials and Democratic legislators provide for their own children. This ongoing atrocity affects millions of children every year. The Chicago strike was one more outrage in a long history of outrages against the most vulnerable members of society. Republicans deplored the strike but never put a face on its minority victims.[22]

Virtually every city council and every school board and every school district in America's large inner cities is 100 percent controlled by Democrats and has been for more than fifty years. Democrats are responsible for everything that is wrong in these inner cities and their schools that policy can affect. Democrats are crushing the life out of millions of poor black and Hispanic children. But Republicans wouldn't think of mentioning it.

At the 2012 Republican convention, one keynote speaker did refer to the teacher unions and their opposition to tying teacher rewards to performance. That speaker was Governor Chris Christie of New Jersey, probably the most aggressive and articulate Republican elected official. But here is how Christie framed his criticism:

> We [Republicans] believe that the majority of teachers in America know our system must be reformed to put students first so

that America can compete.... We believe that we should honor and reward the good ones while doing what's best for our nation's future—demanding accountability, higher standards and the best teacher in every classroom.

They believe the educational establishment will always put themselves ahead of children. That self-interest trumps common sense. They believe in pitting unions against teachers, educators against parents, and lobbyists against children. They believe in teachers' unions.

And that's all he said. The issues are there—accountability, standards, and rewards for teacher performance. The policy is there. But how tepid and anodyne is the expression. Where is the moral outrage? Where are the young, mainly minority victims of this abuse by the unions and the Democratic Party? Where is the naming of the culprits? It is not the "educational establishment" that is ruining the lives and blocking the opportunities of African American and Hispanic children. It's the Democratic Party. Democrats are the educational establishment in every failing public school district. The Democrat teacher unions and the party that supports them are destroying the lives of African American and Hispanic students. But you would never know it from listening to Governor Christie.

Democrats will go to the wall to prevent poor parents from getting vouchers to provide their children the same quality education that well-heeled Democratic legislators and union executives provide for theirs. This is a moral scandal. It is an issue of fairness to get angry about. Politically, it could drive a crippling wedge through the Democratic base. Where is the Republican who is making the case?

Defending a failed school system for poor, mainly black and Hispanic, children is merely the most obvious way that Democrats are harming America's vulnerable communities. Subverting family structures through a misconceived welfare system, encouraging food stamp dependency, providing monetary incentives to bring children into this world who have no prospect of a decent life—these are the corrupt fruits of Democratic policies that are spiraling out of control. Republicans criticize the handout programs as "wasteful." They need to start attacking them as morally repulsive, life-destroying programs that are inhumane and unjust.

Republicans need to keep in mind that the Democrats' primary agenda is not to promote practical solutions to complex problems. If it were, they would not continually promote programs that have failed, particularly those that have crippled millions of lives. The Democrats' only consistent agenda is *power*, which they hope to use to fundamentally transform America into a guardian state. To achieve their goal, they constantly work to extend government control, threatening the individual freedom of every American. And they demonize their opponents as enemies of progress, of social justice, and of minority rights. The only way to counter such attacks is by turning the Democrats' guns around—by exposing them as the agents of injustice and exploiters of the most vulnerable, by treating them as the reactionary proponents of policies that are bankrupt and that have proved destructive wherever they have been put in place.

CHAPTER TWO

DEFEND OUR COUNTRY

Republicans have been a minority party for all but twelve of the years since the Second World War. In election after election, voters have preferred Democratic promoters of the welfare state over Republican proponents of fiscal restraint. But the same electorate has reversed itself and crossed party lines to support Republicans when it came to protecting the American homeland. In a majority of postwar presidential elections where national security was a primary issue, voters cast their presidential ballots for a Republican.

While voters gave Democrats a majority in the House for forty of forty-two years during America's Cold War with the Soviet Union, they preferred a Republican as their commander in chief for twenty-eight of those years. Three of the four Democrats who made it to the White House—Truman, Kennedy, and Johnson—were strong anti-Communists and military hawks, holding views indistinguishable from most Republicans on national security. The fourth, Jimmy Carter, was a former naval officer and beneficiary of the Watergate scandal. He was also a foreign policy disaster who served only one term before being defeated by Ronald Reagan. In all the years from 1945 to the present, the only Republican presidential victory in which national security did not play a major role was George W. Bush's in 2000, and in that election Bush lost the popular vote.

In sum, when Republicans win national elections, it is because the American people trust them with the nation's security and don't trust their Democratic opponents. The issue of national security, moreover, has unified Republicans themselves. The party is a diverse coalition, and its factions are capable of sitting out elections if their favored issues don't receive the desired attention. But concern for the nation's safety has historically united the disparate elements of the Republican coalition. When the security of the country is a major issue in a national campaign, it pushes other divisive issues into the background.

The conventional wisdom of Republican consultants is "It's the economy, stupid," although it was a Democrat who actually came up with that phrase. But the lesson of postwar electoral history is clear: Republicans win national elections only when they put national security issues at the center of their campaigns.

Putting national security in the political foreground should not be difficult in a post-9/11 world in which Americans have been attacked on American soil, the number of countries openly supporting Islamist terror has steadily grown, and the most dangerous Islamist regime—Iran—is relentlessly pursuing nuclear weapons. Global turmoil in the election year of 2012—governments falling to Islamist parties in the Middle East and violent conflicts erupting across the region—should have made national security a priority for both parties. Indeed, the international situation as the election approached provided eerie parallels to the early Cold War conflicts, with implications equally dire. Yet Republicans failed to make these threats a political issue, while Democrats, abetted by a compliant media, were only too happy to pretend they were under control.

To appreciate fully the disorientation of the Republican Party in 2012, recall how prominent national security concerns actually were as the election approached. In the four years since Obama's inauguration, almost *three times* as many Americans were killed in Afghanistan as in the eight years that Bush conducted the war, and there was no prospect of victory. Under

Obama's failed leadership, there were more than eight thousand Islamic terrorist attacks on "infidels" across the globe.[1] This represented a 25 percent increase over the years in which the fighting in Iraq was at its height. In the face of this bloody Islamist offensive, Obama was actually claiming that the war against al Qaeda was essentially won and the terrorist threat subsiding: "Al Qaeda is on the path to defeat and Osama bin Laden is dead."[2]

The Obama administration had officially dropped the term "Global War on Terror" in favor of the Orwellian euphemism "overseas contingency operations."[3] This deceptive formula was a practical implementation of its policy of denying the religious nature of the Islamic war against the West and of minimizing the Islamist threat. Denial was also evident in Obama's treatment of the Middle East's most dangerous actor and chief sponsor of terrorism, Iran. Obama was silent when hundreds of thousands of Iranians poured into the streets of the capital in 2009, during the "Green Revolution," to call for an end to the dictatorship. While Iran supplied jihadists with the improvised explosive devices responsible for most of the American fatalities in Iraq, Obama was uncomfortable with the anti-regime protesters because he was eager for rapprochement with the terrorist regime. His administration not only dragged its feet on sanctions designed to halt Iran's nuclear program but actually worked to limit them.

A particularly egregious example of the administration's policy toward the Islamic jihad was its response to the 2009 massacre of thirteen unarmed soldiers at Fort Hood by a Muslim fanatic (who three years later had still not been brought to trial). The Fort Hood terrorist had successfully infiltrated the U.S. Army and, despite open expressions of hatred for the West and a calling card that identified him as a "Soldier of Islam," had been promoted to the rank of major. The Obama administration was unconcerned with the infiltration of its military by a self-declared enemy and even refused to recognize the shootings as a terrorist act, classifying the attack as "workplace violence."[4] But neither the troubling implications of these official cover-ups nor the facts about the growing Islamist threats were features of the Republican presidential campaign. On the contrary, Mitt Romney focused almost exclusively on the economy, appointing as his "director of foreign, defense, and judicial policy" a thirty-year-old novice named Alex Wong, who had graduated from Harvard Law School only the year before.[5]

In 2012, Republicans were handed an "October surprise" that provided them with a prime opportunity to address the issue. On the anniversary of 9/11, Islamic jihadists launched attacks against the American embassies in Egypt and other countries. In Libya, al Qaeda terrorists overran an American consular compound in Benghazi, murdering the American ambassador and three brave members of his staff, including two Navy SEALs. The attack took place in a country that had recently been destabilized by Obama's unauthorized military intervention against the regime of Muammar Gaddafi. As a senator, Obama had denounced the military intervention in Iraq, which had been authorized by both houses of Congress. As president, he invoked the principle of non-intervention to justify his passivity in the face of governmental atrocities in Syria and Iran. But in Libya—without notifying Congress or even members of his own party—he set in motion the invasion of a country that posed no threat to the United States. Obama's unilateral military intervention led directly to the rise of the local al Qaeda, which planted its flag atop the same American compound it later destroyed.

President Obama learned about the Benghazi attack within its first hour; the battle would last for another six. The embattled Americans inside the compound begged for help from U.S. military assets, which were stationed only an hour or two away. But an order to "stand down" was given, and help was denied. No one, not even the secretary of defense, could locate the president for the duration of the battle. This was one of the most shameful acts in the history of the American presidency. It was compounded when Obama's team then went into cover-up mode, hiding for weeks the fact that what had happened was a terrorist attack, pretending that it was the result of a spontaneous demonstration over an anti-Mohammed video posted on the internet. This was the thrust of Obama's speech to the United Nations two weeks later when he paid tribute to his slain ambassador but decried "a crude and disgusting video [that] sparked outrage throughout the Muslim world," covering up that it was a carefully planned terrorist attack by an organization he had claimed was on the verge of defeat.[6]

Before his overthrow, Gaddafi had warned that his removal would unleash the forces of Islamic jihad not only in Libya but throughout North Africa—a prophecy that was quickly realized. In the aftermath of Obama's aggression, al Qaeda was able to take control of an area twice the size of Germany in the African state of Mali. Jihadists emerged as the ruling parties in Tunisia and Egypt with the acquiescence and even the assistance of the Obama administration. A savage civil war erupted in Syria, killing tens of thousands and pitting a fascist regime allied with Iran against rebel forces aligned with al Qaeda and the Muslim Brotherhood.

As these disasters unfolded, the White House not only failed to oppose the Islamists, it armed and enabled them—in the case of Egypt, with hundreds of millions of dollars in military aid and F-16 bomber jets. The Muslim Brotherhood government in Egypt, the largest and most important country in the Middle East, was a direct product of Obama's intervention. He had called for the removal of its pro-American ruler, Hosni Mubarak, and then promoted the Brotherhood's ascension to power by portraying it as a "moderate" actor in the democratic process.[7] As the situation in the region deteriorated, the chief beneficiary of America's financial, diplomatic, and military support was the Brotherhood, which was the driving force behind the Islamist jihad, the creator of Hamas, and the spawner of al Qaeda.

To allay concerns about the emergence of the Brotherhood, Obama's secretary of state, Hillary Clinton, declared: "We believe…that it is in the interests of the United States to engage with all parties that are peaceful, and committed to non-violence, that intend to compete for the parliament and the presidency."[8] Here she was referring to an organization whose spiritual leader, Yusuf al-Qaradawi, had recently called for a second Holocaust of the Jews—"Allah willing, at the hands of the believers"—and a party that was calling for the establishment of a Muslim caliphate in Jerusalem and the destruction of the Jewish state.[9]

Soon after Clinton's endorsement, the Muslim Brotherhood's presidential candidate, Mohammed Morsi, was elected Egypt's new leader. Secure in the support of the Obama White House, he wasted no time in abolishing the constitution and instituting a dictatorship. There was no serious protest from the United States. Only months before the burial of what was left of Egypt's democracy, the new dictator received a visit from the chairman of the Senate Foreign Relations Committee, John Kerry. The man who would soon succeed Clinton as secretary of state assured Americans, "In our discussions, Mr. Morsi committed to protecting fundamental freedoms, including women's rights, minority rights, the right to free expression and assembly, and he said he understood the importance of Egypt's post-revolutionary relationships with America and Israel." With unintended irony, the credulous Kerry added, "Ultimately, just as it is anywhere in the world, actions will matter more than words."[10]

Just as Obama misread Egypt and Libya, so he misread Syria. Both Clinton and Kerry praised the country's dictator, Bashar al-Assad, as a political reformer and friend of democracy just as he was preparing to launch a war against his own people. Meeting with Assad, Kerry insisted that the Syrian was "an essential player in bringing peace and stability to the region."[11] Shortly thereafter, Assad launched a series of massacres that left tens of thousands of Syrians dead and provoked international calls for a humanitarian intervention—calls that Obama simply ignored.

During the last months of the 2012 campaign, Obama's policies were imploding all over the Middle East. His claim that al Qaeda was on the run had been brutally exposed as hollow. His administration was supporting an Islamist party in Egypt that, with his help, had taken over the most important country in the Middle East. He was steadily moving away from America's principal ally in the region, Israel, and toward America's most threatening enemy, Iran. Yet in the face of these developments, with their ominous implications for America's future, the Republican presidential campaign was all but silent about national security.

THE PROBLEM IS THE CULTURE OF THE REPUBLICAN PARTY

In his acceptance speech at the Republican National Convention in Tampa, Mitt Romney failed to mention the Muslim Middle East and devoted only one sentence to Obama's treatment of Israel, noting that the president had thrown America's only real ally in the region "under the bus." Romney did not address Obama's role as enabler of the Muslim Brotherhood or the millions of dollars his administration had provided to the Palestinian jihadists on the West Bank and in Gaza, whose stated goal was the destruction of the Jewish state. He did not mention the calls by the Islamist leaders of Egypt and Iran for the destruction of the Jews and the completion of the job that Hitler started.

To be fair, Romney did touch on national security issues, but only briefly. First he scolded Obama for abandoning America's East European allies by reneging on a previous commitment to their missile defense. This was followed by approximately 160 words reprimanding Obama for his notorious apologies to America's enemies, then praising him for his order to kill bin Laden (as though this were a difficult choice), and finally regretting that he had failed to take seriously enough Iran's nuclear ambitions. He began these remarks by making foreign policy a subordinate clause of his economic agenda:

> I will begin my presidency with a jobs tour. President Obama began with an apology tour. America, he said, had dictated to other nations. No, Mr. President, America has freed other nations from dictators. Every American was relieved the day President Obama gave the order, and SEAL Team Six took out

Osama bin Laden. But on another front, every American is less secure today because he has failed to slow Iran's nuclear threat.[12]

To begin with, it was the wrong tone. Romney's words did not reflect the urgency or the magnitude of the crisis Obama's policies had created. But more important, the substance of his criticism was deficient. There was no mention of Obama's support for the Muslim Brotherhood, America's sworn enemy, nor was there reference to the disasters of his policies in Libya and Syria or to the betrayals of the principles that Obama and the Democrats had espoused in their attacks on President Bush over Iraq.

While the Romney campaign was devoid of a coherent and sustained foreign policy message, it would be a serious mistake to regard this election debacle as exclusively—or even mainly—the fault of the Republican candidate and his campaign or of the "Republican establishment." The whole party was silent about foreign policy. Super PACs, forbidden by law from communicating with the campaign but deploying hundreds of millions of dollars to shape the anti-Obama message, had also focused on the economy and failed to address the foreign policy disasters of the administration or the national security threats they had magnified by their actions.

The Crossroads super PAC is headed by Karl Rove, who can fairly be linked to a Republican establishment. But Americans for Prosperity, one of the most important super PACs, is outside the party apparatus and culture and represents an independent conservative viewpoint. Yet neither of these super PACs focused on the national security issues in the manner necessary for the Republican to win the election. Everyone on the Republican side agreed that the economy would be the campaign's decisive issue. As is often the case, this conventional wisdom turned out to be wrong. This should not have been a surprise. In 1980, Jimmy Carter had presided over an economy worse than Obama's and was leading the Republican, Ronald Reagan, by seven points in April. It was only when the Iran hostage crisis blew up in his face that he fell behind, after which there was no return.[13]

It is true that Romney made the situation even worse by his strategic decision in the third debate to hug Obama on foreign policy issues. But it is far from certain that any of the other potential Republican nominees would have conducted their campaigns differently. At one time or another, there were a dozen Republican candidates for the nomination, and they participated in nineteen public debates. There were candidates for social conservatism, candidates for fiscal responsibility and job creation, and candidates for libertarian principles and moderate values. But there was not one Republican candidate for an aggressive assault on Obama's disastrous foreign policy.

The failure of Republicans to grab the one issue that had won them virtually all their presidential victories since 1952 could be traced to an event that took place nearly ten years earlier: the Bush administration's failure to defend the Iraq War against the Democrats' underhanded attacks. When the Democrats successfully branded Iraq as a reckless intervention and a bad war, Republicans lost control of the national security narrative and have not regained it since.

The magnitude of the post-Iraq problem is revealed by an incident that took place four months prior to the 2012 election. Representative Michele Bachmann and four other Republican House members sent a letter to the Justice Department's inspector general asking him to look into the possibility of Islamist influence in the Obama administration. The letter expressed concern about State Department policies that "appear to be a result of influence operations conducted by individuals and organizations associated with the Muslim Brotherhood."[14] The letter then listed five specific ways in which Secretary of State Hillary Clinton had actively assisted the Muslim Brotherhood's ascent to power in Egypt, producing a decisive shift in the Middle East toward jihadist Islam.

The Bachmann letter specifically asked for an inquiry into the activities of Hillary Clinton's deputy chief of staff and principal advisor on Muslim affairs, Huma Abedin, whose mother, late father, and brother were all identifiable leaders of the Muslim Brotherhood. For twelve years prior to being hired by Clinton, Abedin had worked for an organization founded and run by a major Muslim Brotherhood figure, Abdullah Omar Naseef, one of the three principal financiers of Osama bin Laden and a figure still wanted by U.S. authorities in connection with 9/11. Abedin's mother also held a high position in the organization, which is dedicated to promoting Islamic supremacist doctrines and creating Muslim majorities in non-Muslim countries. Another important member of the Obama administration with ties to the Muslim Brotherhood was Rashad Hussain, a deputy associate White House counsel with responsibilities for national security and Muslim affairs. And there were others.

The Obama administration's tacit alliance with an Islamist organization like the Muslim Brotherhood was concerning enough, and the presence of identifiable Islamists such as Huma Abedin and Rashad Hussain in positions of influence on matters of national security and Muslim affairs was reasonable grounds for an inquiry.[15] But when Bachmann's letter surfaced, the congresswoman and her colleagues were savagely attacked as "McCarthyites" and "Islamophobes," and their inquiry was rejected as toxic. The attacks came not only from the *Washington Post*, leading Democrats, and such well-known academic apologists for the Brotherhood as Georgetown University's John Esposito, but also from Republicans John McCain and John Boehner. Without bothering to address the facts that Bachmann's letter presented, McCain charged, "When anyone, not least a member of Congress, launches specious and degrading attacks against fellow Americans on the basis of nothing more than fear of who they are, in ignorance of what they stand for, it defames the spirit of our nation, and we all grow poor because of it." Said Boehner, "I don't know Huma, but from everything that I do know of her she has a sterling character. And I think accusations like this being thrown around are pretty dangerous."[16] As a result of these reactions there was no investigation.

The terms "McCarthyite" and "Islamophobe" are bludgeons wielded by the political Left to shut down inquiry into subversive behaviors. The same concern about reckless accusations doesn't seem to apply to leftists, who can get away with baseless claims, for example that President Bush "betrayed us" in Iraq (Al Gore), conducted a war that was "a fraud" (Ted Kennedy) or "lied while people died" (Democrats generally).[17]

The success of these attacks during the Iraq War has left Republicans at a loss for words when it comes to holding Democrats to account over a wide range of security issues. For example, when Obama finally withdrew American troops from Iraq—a country that borders Afghanistan, Syria, and Iran—he failed to negotiate a "status of forces" agreement that would provide for an American base there. The Iraq War cost the United States 35,000 casualties and $3 trillion, yet the terms of Obama's withdrawal left us with no material benefits to show for it. The Left impugned Bush's motives with the malicious slogan "No blood for oil," but we have no access to Iraqi oil. By failing to secure a military base and twenty thousand troops stationed in country, as the Joint Chiefs recommended, Obama undid the gains of the war and surrendered Iraq to the tender mercies of Tehran and the al Qaeda forces still in country.

There was no Republican outrage over this capitulation. No Republican accused Obama of betraying the Americans and Iraqis who gave their lives to keep Iraq free of jihadist influence and out of the clutches of Iran, although that would have been a reasonable charge. As a result, Republicans remained on the defensive, a position painfully evident in the third presidential debate. Here is how Romney attempted to frame the issue and how he was backed down by Obama:

ROMNEY: Number two, with regards to Iraq, you and I agreed, I believe, that there should have been a status of forces agreement. Did you—

OBAMA: That's not true.

ROMNEY: Oh, you didn't—you didn't want a status of forces agreement?

OBAMA: No, but what I—what I would not have done is left ten thousand troops in Iraq that would tie us down. That certainly would not help us in the Middle East....

ROMNEY: ... That was your posture. That was my posture as well. I thought it should have been five thousand troops.... The answer was, we got no troops whatsoever.

OBAMA: This is just a few weeks ago that you indicated that we should still have troops in Iraq.

ROMNEY: No, I didn't. I'm sorry, that's—[18]

Romney not only failed to put Obama on the defensive for having failed to secure a military base, he backed down from even the minimalist suggestion of five thousand troops. He was worried about looking like a "warmonger" or a reckless "neoconservative" for insisting that America should maintain a military presence in a country which thousands of Americans had died to defend and which was strategically situated between Iran and the Arabian Peninsula, the crucible of the Islamist jihad. More important, Romney was not alone. Although the betrayal took place during a presidential election year, no other notable Republican uttered a word of protest.

RECAPTURING THE NATIONAL SECURITY NARRATIVE

The moment Republicans lost the upper hand on national security was in June 2003, just three months into the war in Iraq and only six weeks after the U.S.-led coalition forces had toppled the Saddam regime. That month, the Democratic Party launched a national campaign against America's commander in chief, claiming that he had lied to the American people to lure them into a war that was "unnecessary," "immoral," and "illegal."

Until that moment, the conflict in Iraq had been supported by both parties and was regarded by both as a strategic necessity in the war launched by Islamic terrorists on 9/11. Saddam Hussein had launched two aggressive wars in the Middle East, murdered three hundred thousand Iraqis, used chemical weapons on his own citizens, and put in place a nuclear weapons program, thwarted only by his defeat in the 1991 Gulf War. Over the next decade, his regime defied sixteen United Nations Security Council resolutions attempting to enforce the Gulf War truce and stop him from pursuing weapons of mass destruction. In September 2002, the Security Council added a seventeenth resolution, which gave Saddam until December 7 to comply with its terms or face consequences. When Iraq failed to comply, Bush made the only decision compatible with the preservation of international law and the security of the United States by launching a preemptive invasion to remove the regime. Two days prior to the invasion, the Iraqi dictator was given the option of leaving the country and averting the war. He rejected the offer, and a U.S.-led coalition entered the country on March 19, 2003.[19]

The attacks of 9/11 had been made possible because of the safe harbor provided by a rogue state, Afghanistan. In response, President Bush had declared that America would regard as enemies any regime providing support for terrorists. Iraq was such a regime. Removing Saddam had been an official U.S. policy since October 1998, when a Democratic president, Bill Clinton, signed the Iraq Liberation Act.[20] Bush's decision to use force in Iraq was authorized by both houses of Congress, including a majority of Democrats in the Senate. It was supported with eloquent speeches by John Kerry, John Edwards, Al Gore, and other Democratic leaders. But in June 2003, just three months after the fighting began, the Democrats turned against the war and launched a five-year campaign to delegitimize it, casting America and its Republican leaders as the villains. This betrayal of the nation and its troops on the battlefield was unprecedented. Major press institutions following the Democrats' lead conducted a propaganda campaign against the war, blowing up minor incidents like the misbehavior of guards at the Abu Ghraib prison into international scandals, which damaged America's prestige and weakened its morale. The *New York Times* and the *Washington Post* leaked classified documents, destroying three major national security programs designed to protect Americans from terrorist attacks.[21] Every day of the war, there was front-page coverage of America's body counts in Iraq and Afghanistan designed to sap America's will to fight. (Such coverage disappeared with the advent of the Obama administration even though the wars and the body counts continued.) The media fueled a massive "antiwar" movement, which attacked America's presence in Iraq and its conduct of the war in the most damning terms. The Democrats' break with the postwar tradition of bipartisanship in foreign policy was all the more unpalatable because they had authorized and supported the war in the first place.

But Republicans didn't lose control of the national security narrative merely because Democrats betrayed a war they had encouraged. They lost it because they never held the Democrats to account for their betrayal. They never suggested that the Democrats' attacks on the war were deceitful and unpatriotic and jeopardized American lives. They never answered the Democrats' attacks by exposing their hypocrisy or by characterizing their reckless accusations against the administration as sabotage of the war effort. Fear of the media's reaction even kept the Bush Justice Department from indicting those who had leaked classified information, though they had clearly violated the Espionage Act. No Republican accused Democrats of conducting a campaign to demoralize America's troops in the field, even when Senator John Kerry, during a 2004 presidential debate, called it "the wrong war in the wrong place at the wrong time."[22] How must those words have sounded to a nineteen-year-old Marine facing down Islamic terrorists in Fallujah? The word "betrayal" was never used by the White House to describe the Democrats who undermined the war effort. But it *was* used by Democrats like Al Gore to characterize President Bush.

The Republicans' failure to defend the war they had led turned a good war into a bad war. It turned a disloyal opposition into a patriotic movement, with dramatic consequences for the future. If the war against a monster like Saddam could not be prosecuted without dividing the nation, then American resistance to any terror-supporting rogue state could be portrayed as reckless and unjustifiable aggression. In losing the political war over Iraq, Republicans lost the national security narrative, which is why they are tongue-tied today when it comes to issues of war and peace. Call it the "Iraq War Syndrome."

And so when the Republican presidential nominee, John McCain, suggested during the 2008 campaign that maintaining troops in a postwar Iraq was a prudent measure, Barack Obama simply ridiculed him: "You know, John McCain wants to continue a war in Iraq perhaps as long as a hundred years."[23] As though America were responsible for 9/11 and the jihad directed at its citizens. This refrain became a constant theme of the winning Obama campaign—*Republicans will involve us in more Iraqs.*

Three years later, when Obama delivered Iraq to Iran, no Republican accused him of betraying the Americans who gave their lives to make Iraq independent and free. And in the 2012 presidential campaign, Romney was unable to make the case for even five thousand troops, even though Iraq had by then actually fallen under the sway of Iran and was providing a land conduit for Iranian weapons headed for the Syrian civil war. Although the purpose of the wars in Afghanistan and Iraq was to deny safe harbors to terrorists, there are now nearly a dozen such harbors, including Lebanon, Turkey, Syria, Mali, Iran, Egypt, Somalia, Yemen, and Palestine. Far from considering these terror-supporting states hostile, the White House is providing several of them with economic and military aid. The United States is not only losing the war against enemies whose stated goal is its destruction, it is led by an appeasement party that is making the situation worse by the day. At the end of 2013, Obama openly sided with the Iranian axis against America's allies Israel and Saudi Arabia by ending sanctions designed to deny Iran a nuclear arsenal. The only way to reverse this dangerous trend is for Republicans to renew their role as guardians of the nation's security, to educate the electorate about the threat posed by Islamic supremacists, and to challenge the Democrats' seditious efforts to appease their malign agendas. It is also Republicans' only path to an electoral majority.

CHAPTER THREE

CHAPTER THREE

THE PROGRESSIVE THREAT

I was born at the beginning of the Second World War to parents who were high school teachers and members of the Communist Party. They called themselves "progressives" and were believers in "social justice." The movement to which they belonged was dedicated to the destruction of their country, although they would never have looked at it that way, and so-called liberals would still be the first to deny it.[1] In those days, American schools were old-fashioned enough that my parents did not use their classrooms to indoctrinate students in their radical politics and anti-American agendas as tens of thousands of university professors and K–12 teachers do today.[2] In their public lives, they hid their real goals behind the fashionable progressive issues of the time—"civil rights," "peace," and "equality." The issues were never really the issues for them. The issue was always the socialist future and the revolution that was going to bring it about.

A crucial fact for understanding the current political situation is that the cause to which my parents were dedicated and the conspiracy to which they belonged have steadily migrated to the heart of the Democratic Party, and now, in the persons of Barack Obama and his closest advisors, they occupy the Oval Office. Obama; his chief political operative, Valerie Jarrett; and his chief political strategist, David Axelrod, were all raised and trained in the same Communist progressive Left as I was, and all have remained heart and soul a part of it.[3]

I can say this with the confidence of someone who turned his back on that destructive movement. If someone has supported an idea or movement that he comes to see as destructive, the first thing he will want to do when he abandons it is to repudiate it and warn others against it. If he does not do that, it is apparent that he has not left the movement or abandoned the idea but has just put another face on the same destructive goals. Instead of calling himself a Communist or socialist, he will call himself a liberal and progressive. In fact, as I have just noted, this camouflage is very old. As a young man, I never heard my parents or their Communist Party friends refer to themselves as Communists. They were progressives.

Ever since Barack Obama was elected president and began his radical course, American conservatives have been in a state of shock, as though they can't quite believe what is taking place. Until Obama began implementing his agenda and revealing his methods, conservatives regularly colluded in the illusion that unrepentant radicals and dedicated socialists and intolerant progressives were simply "liberals." What is liberal about progressives except their attitudes toward sex, drugs, and America's adversaries?

Today, the progressive juggernaut is systematically bankrupting the nation and undoing its constitutional arrangements. Beginning with the determination to ram through the most comprehensive, invasive, and coercive legislation in the nation's history, the contempt of the ruling party for consultative government has been relentlessly on display. During the impasse leading to a government shutdown, the Senate majority leader, Harry Reid, defended his refusal to negotiate with Republicans in these words: "We are here to support the federal government. That's our job."[4] Forget about representing the people. Forget what America is about.

Democrats have steadily moved the country in the direction of a one-party state. If you have transformed the taxing agency of the government into a political weapon (and Obama has), if you are setting up a massive government program to collect the financial and health information of every citizen and control his access to care, and if you have in place a spy agency that can monitor the communications of every citizen, you don't really need a secret police to destroy your political opponents. You already have the means to do it. And once you have silenced them, you can proceed with your plans to remake the world in your image.

The good news is that the excesses of the Obama administration have aroused a sleeping giant. For the first time since the Cold War, ordinary Americans, who didn't see this coming and couldn't imagine that it would, are calling socialists by their right name, and conservatives are finally organizing the grassroots to defend their freedom. Thanks to the Tea Parties, congressional leaders have emerged who are willing to stand up to the intimidating tactics of the Left and not back down.

HOW PROGRESSIVES THINK (OR DON'T)

In confronting the Left, conservatives should not make the mistake of assuming that progressives share our understanding of society's problems, merely differing about the practical steps needed to address them. No one should think that progressives want to see our communities prosper within the framework that has defined America since its inception and provided its blessings. The nature of the progressive outlook inspires contempt for the American past and disdain for America's social contract, which it regards as tainted by racism, sexism, and imperial ambition.

To circumvent the Founders' designs, progressives have come up with the idea of a "living constitution," which they can alter at will.[5] Justice Ruth Bader Ginsburg of the U.S. Supreme Court recently provided a glimpse of how progressives would alter the Constitution. When the Muslim Brotherhood ascended to power in Egypt with the help of the Obama administration, in 2012, its leaders pretended to be interested in adopting a new constitution to please their White House promoters. This was an Orwellian charade, for the Muslim Brotherhood already has a constitution. Its motto proclaims, "Allah is our goal, the Koran is our constitution...."[6] When asked for her advice about a new constitution for Egypt, Justice Ginsburg went along with the charade rather than expose it. She would not recommend the American Constitution as a model, she said, because it is "old." She would recommend the constitution of South Africa instead.[7]

It was a revealing choice. The South African constitution reflects the Communist outlook of the leaders of the African National Congress who wrote it and provides as much protection for South Africans as the notorious Stalinist constitution did for the citizens of Soviet Russia. Like its Soviet counterpart, the South African constitution is made up of "paper rights," as James Madison would have dismissed them.[8] These are rights that either cannot be enforced or can easily be withdrawn. For example, the South African constitution includes "the right to be protected against violence." Despite this guarantee, South Africa has a murder rate *seven times* that of the United States and is the rape capital of the world.[9] The South African constitution also provides citizens with the right not to be discriminated against on the basis of race or sex—*unless* the government decides such discrimination is fair. Lest anyone think I exaggerate, here is the text itself: "Discrimination on one or more of the grounds listed in subsection (3) is unfair unless it is established that the discrimination is fair."[10]

While the South African constitution does "protect" the right to property, that right survives only until the government decides that expropriation is necessary "under a law of general application" to promote the common good. In other words, the right to own property exists until social justice demands that it doesn't. The South African constitution is not a democratic constitution any more than Stalin's constitution was. Yet the progressive Justice Ginsburg regards it as superior to the one America's Founders crafted.

When Justice Ginsburg proclaimed the superiority of the South African constitution over our own, the only outrage came from conservatives. Not a word of protest emerged from her three progressive colleagues on the Court, or from Democrats, or from so-called liberals generally. As they all know, America's constitutional rights are expressed not as socialist entitlements but as *restrictions* on government—"Congress shall make no law...."

The rights of Americans—the rights that secure their freedom—are bestowed not by government, which could then take them away, but "by their *Creator*." The conviction that individual rights are derived from "Nature's God" and not from the state is what separates America's Constitution from the constitutions of tyrannical regimes.[11]

How could a U.S. Supreme Court justice, sworn to uphold the Constitution, be so alienated from its fundamental principles? How could her Democratic colleagues be so alienated from the Founders' creed? It's because they are *progressives*. For guidance on policy, progressives draw their inspiration from an imaginary future where social justice prevails. That is why they reject America's outdated social contract and the wisdom it embodies. In other words, they do not share political values with conservatives, who cherish the American idea of liberty and are vigilant in defending it.

A defining characteristic of the progressive outlook is its belief in the doctrine of original innocence. The modern source of this belief is the French radical Jean-Jacques Rousseau, who maintained that private property is the cause of social evils and that "Man is born free but is everywhere in chains."[12] This is a doctrine so obviously false it hardly needs refutation, except that progressives believe it. What they believe is that "society" is the root cause of social problems. In their view, human beings are naturally cooperative and sharing, honest and moral, but are corrupted by social institutions that encourage prejudice and greed and set them against each other. They believe that "social justice" is the model of how human beings naturally relate to each other, that equality and cooperation reflect human nature, and that socialism is therefore the name of a truly human future.

Conservatives believe the opposite. They believe that human beings are the root cause of social problems and that social institutions are corrupt because human beings create and run them. It is the barbarity of the species that requires the intervention of a social order with the disciplines of morality and law to civilize its inhabitants. This is also what the Founders believed. It is why they did not create a pure democracy that would express the popular will, which they regarded as unruly, emotion driven, and dangerous.

Instead they devised a system of checks and balances to frustrate the majority's natural instinct to tyrannize the weak and outnumbered. And they set limits to government.

This is a difference in outlooks as profound as the gulf that separated the sides in the Cold War between communism and freedom. It is in fact the same gulf. Progressives do not openly call for the creation of a totalitarian state, but that is the logic of their desire: to compel people to do what is good for them, down to the last Big Gulp. Lenin and the Bolsheviks did not set out to create a gulag state that would execute millions and crush human liberty. Quite the contrary. The Bolsheviks proposed to feed the hungry and care for the helpless and usher in the "kingdom of freedom."[13] But their plan to accomplish this dream required that they transform human nature, and that project led them inexorably down the totalitarian path. If you believe that the cause of human suffering is "society," and if you believe that by fundamentally transforming society you can change human nature and end human suffering and need, what means will you deny yourself, what opposition will you not suppress, to see that the transformation takes place?

Because progressives see themselves as social redeemers and their goal as saving the world, they regard politics as a religious war. This is why they are intolerant toward those who disagree with them and who stand in the way of their "solutions." It is why they exclude conservatives from the educational institutions they control. It is why the politics of personal destruction is their politics of choice and why they can commit character assassinations without regrets. Obama never apologized for accusing his opponent of killing a cancer patient during the election campaign, because saving humanity means never having to say you're sorry.

PROGRESSIVE ENDS AND MEANS

If changing social institutions is the path to salvation, then the only obstacle to a world of harmony and plenty is the attitude of those who oppose progressive schemes—in other words, conservatives. Without conservatives, in this view, the world would be an incomparably better place. Conservatives, therefore, are not just wrongheaded; as progressives view them, they are reactionary and evil. Conservative opposition to progressive schemes is the cause of human suffering and want. That is why intolerance toward conservatives is justified, because the end justifies the means.

"Whenever we think about social change, the question of means and ends arises," writes Obama's political mentor, Saul Alinsky, in his *Rules for Radicals*.[14] "The man of action views the issue of means and ends in pragmatic and strategic terms…. He asks of ends only whether they are achievable and worth the cost; of means, only whether they will work." But what if the means are immoral, or criminal? Won't that corrupt the cause itself? Not in Alinsky's view. "To say that corrupt means corrupt the ends is to believe in the immaculate conception of ends and principles. The real arena is corrupt and bloody. Life is a corrupting process…. [H]e who fears corruption fears life."[15] To the progressive whose conscience considers certain means unacceptable, Alinsky answers, "One does not always enjoy the luxury of a decision that is consistent both with one's individual conscience and the good of mankind. The choice must always be for the latter." In other words, it is the obligation of progressives to dispense with moral scruples when committing crimes for the benefit of mankind.

People on the Left may be delusional, but they are not stupid. They know what they can say and get away with and what they can't. That is why Communists in the circles I frequented in my youth never identified themselves as Communists but always as "progressives" and "Jeffersonian democrats" (which is the last thing they were). In Stalin's day, the goal of the Communist Party was a "dictatorship of the proletariat" and a "Soviet America." But under Stalin's inspiration, the official Communist slogan was "Peace, Jobs, and Democracy."

Dishonesty is endemic to the progressive cause because its radical goals cannot be admitted; the dishonesty is a cultural inheritance, instinctive and indispensable. It is no coincidence that Barack Obama, a born-and-bred leftist, is the most compulsive and brazen liar ever to occupy the White House. His true agenda is radical and unpalatable, and therefore he needs to lie about it. What other presidential candidate could have successfully explained away his close association for twenty years with an anti-American racist, Jeremiah Wright, and an anti-American terrorist, William Ayers? Who but the ignorant and the progressively blind could have believed him?

The radical sixties were something of an aberration in that its activists were uncharacteristically candid about their goals. A generation of "new leftists" was rebelling against its Stalinist parents, who had pretended to be liberals to hide their real beliefs and save their political skins. New leftists despised what they thought was the cowardice behind this camouflage. As a "New Left," they were determined to say what they thought and blurt out their desires: "We want a revolution, and we want it *now*." They were actually rather decent to warn others about what they intended. But when they revealed their goals, they set off alarms and therefore didn't get very far.

Those who remained committed to leftist goals after the sixties learned from their experience. They learned to lie. The strategy of the lie became the new progressive gospel. It is what Alinsky's *Rules for Radicals* is really about.[16] Alinsky understood the mistake sixties radicals had made. His message at the time, and to the generations who came after, is easily summarized: Don't telegraph your goals; infiltrate the Democratic Party and other liberal institutions and subvert them; treat moral principles as dispensable fictions; and never forget that your political agenda is not the achievement of this or that reform but political *power* to achieve the socialist goal. The issue is never the issue. The issue is always power—how to wring power out of the democratic process, how to turn the political process into an instrument of control, how to use that control to fundamentally transform the United States of America, which is exactly what Barack Obama, on the eve of his election, warned he would do.

The legislative instrument Obama and the Democrats chose to begin this transformation with was the deliberately misnamed "Patient Protection and Affordable Care Act"—Obamacare.[17] It was presented disingenuously as an act of charity, a plan to cover the thirty million Americans who lacked medical insurance (whether by necessity or by choice). That was the "issue," as the progressives deceptively presented it, and only the first of the calculated lies used to promote it. Among these lies, subsequently exposed, were Obama's claims that government-imposed healthcare would cost less and that every American could keep his health insurance plan if he liked it.[18] This was the lie that said, "We're not going to mess with American freedom." It was a denial that Obamacare is a government-imposed collectivist scheme and that its real goal—"single payer"—will mean healthcare by and for the state and the end of individual choice in matters concerning life and death.[19]

Obamacare is the first stage of an attempt to take control of the life of every American citizen and lay the foundations of a socialist state. This is the reason that none of the promises Obama made about Obamacare was true, beginning with his principal campaign lie that he would not support a program to put the government in charge of healthcare. Obamacare will not cover thirty million uninsured Americans, as Obama said it would; Obamacare will not lower healthcare costs, as Obama and the Democrats promised (it will force taxpayers to subsidize the costs of those who can't afford its expensive price tag); Obamacare is a massive new tax, as they all swore it would never be.

All the promises Obama and the Democrats made about Obamacare were false. They were false because if Obama and the Democrats had been honest about the socialist goals of Obamacare, Americans would never have supported it. There were many ways to correct the problems in the health-care system, to make care more affordable, and to cover the uninsured. Tort reform, medical savings accounts, and interstate competition among insurance companies are three obvious reforms that would have greatly improved matters. A pool for people with preexisting conditions is another. But reforming healthcare using these approaches would not accomplish what the progressives really wanted, which was government control—to subordinate the individual and the private sector to the power of the state. They could not sell such a program to the electorate, so they concealed their goals and brushed aside the reforms that didn't advance them. That was why they shut out their Republican colleagues in Congress and rammed through their nation-transforming legislation on a strict party-line vote. Previously enacted comprehensive reforms—Social Security and Medicare—were passed with overwhelming bipartisan majorities. Everyone understands that in a democracy it is only through consensus that system-wide problems can be corrected. But Obamacare was never about correcting problems. It was always about concentrating power in the hands of the state.

Dishonesty is fundamental to the progressive cause since the cause is always about an imagined future whose panaceas cannot pass the test of experience. Like socialism, socialized medicine has failed wherever it has been tried. Consequently, it can be sold only as something it is not, and its proponents can never tell the truth.

PROGRESSIVES AND PATRIOTISM

Allegiance to an ideal (but impossible) future leads to an alienation from the present, and thus from one's country.[20] Asking progressives about their patriotic feeling makes them uncomfortable. They will tell you they prefer to think of themselves as "members of humanity" or "citizens of the world," an identity that fancy Harvard professors endorse.[21] Progressives are so alienated from their country that they are in some sense foreigners. They are hostile to its history and to its core values, which they see as bulwarks of a society that is guilty of racism and oppression and imperial aggression. And they are emphatically opposed to its constitutional arrangements, which the Framers designed to thwart "wicked projects" that would redistribute income and share individual wealth.

Because conservatives live in the real world, they have trouble imagining that people as privileged by America's generosity as Barack Obama and his entourage of despoilers could be so alienated from their country as to feel *in* it but not *of* it. Justice Ginsburg's dismissive comments about our "old" Constitution are one example of this attitude, but it was expressed most shockingly in the president's actions during the Benghazi attack of September 11, 2012.[22] In the first ninety minutes of the attack, Obama was informed by the secretary of defense that his ambassador was missing and that brave men under his command were fighting for their lives and requesting his help.[23] These men had heroically served their country for more than a decade. They were asking for military assistance and would continue to fight for the next five and a half hours. But their commander in chief hung up the phone, made himself unavailable for the duration of the battle, and left those men to die.

How could an American do that? No one with an ounce of patriotic feeling could have let more than five hours pass without inquiring about the fate of those men. Even Alexei Kosygin, a premier of the Soviet dictatorship, maintained contact with his astronaut as he burned up in space. But America's president, when his soldiers were fighting for their lives, hung up the phone and (presumably) went to bed, flying to Las Vegas the next morning for a campaign fundraiser with the singers Beyoncé and Jay-Z. He did take the time to leave orders that administration spokesmen should tell the American people and the world that the ambassador and his defenders had perished not in a terrorist attack but in a protest provoked by a film that had insulted the prophet Mohammed—a deliberate lie. After a year of stonewalling, there are still no answers to the critical questions as to why Ambassador Christopher Stevens was in Benghazi in the first place, why U.S. forces in the region were ordered to stand down, why the administration lied about what had happened, why there wasn't adequate security, and why the president and the secretary of state abandoned their posts while the attack was in progress. The only administration answer to these questions is the exasperated comment of Secretary of State Clinton, "What difference, at this point, does it make?"[24]

America is now confronted by mortal enemies—Iran, Syria, al Qaeda, the Muslim Brotherhood, Hezbollah, Hamas, and other terrorist armies. These enemies declare that America is the "Great Satan" and should be erased from the face of the earth. Their leaders direct crowds of hundreds of thousands in chants of "Death to America." How can an American president set out to appease them, as Obama consistently has done? How in the face of such threats can he conspire to make his country an object of international derision, no longer respected by its friends, no longer feared by its foes? How could an American leader be so cavalier about having failed so miserably to defend his country's security and uphold its honor? How could he snub its Israeli allies and at the same time grovel before its Islamic enemies? How could he create a vacuum in the Middle East allowing America's old Cold War enemy, Russia, to become the new regional power? How could he ally himself with the Muslim Brotherhood, which slaughters Christians, promises the extermination of the Jews, and spawns America-hating terrorist armies like al Qaeda and Hamas?

The answer to all these questions is astonishing but simple: Obama doesn't identify with his country. He sees himself as a "citizen of the world" and a redresser of the suffering he imagines America has inflicted on its adversaries. If America is the cause of international problems, then weakening America is both progressive and good.

BETRAYAL

The way the Democrats betrayed the war in Iraq provides a revealing insight into the progressive faith. In opposing the war, Democrats condemned America's commander in chief for acting unilaterally, deceptively, and in haste and for thrusting the nation into an unnecessary and illegal war. Those were the issues as the Democrats framed them. But every one of the charges was false. The policy to remove the regime in Iraq was not decided in haste and did not originate with President Bush. It was put in place by a Democratic president, Bill Clinton, when he signed the Iraq Liberation Act, in 1998—five years before Bush sent U.S. troops into Iraq—and fired 450 missiles into that country, more than had been fired during the entire 1991 Gulf War.[25] Clinton launched the missiles unilaterally and without authorization from Congress or consultation with NATO or the

United Nations. His unauthorized aggression against Iraq was supported by Al Gore, John Kerry, and all the Democratic leaders who later attacked Bush.

Ten months before the U.S. invasion of Iraq, Bush warned Saddam to observe the terms of the truce he had signed in 1991 and had repeatedly violated over the following ten years—most disturbingly by impeding UN inspectors' ability to determine if he was still acquiring weapons of mass destruction. Seven months before the invasion, Bush went personally to the United Nations and secured a unanimous Security Council ultimatum to Saddam. UN Resolution 1441 ordered Saddam to comply by December 7, 2002, or face "serious consequences."[26] Two months before that deadline, Bush requested authorization from Congress to use force if Saddam rejected an ultimatum. Both houses of Congress—including a majority of Democrats in the Senate—voted to authorize the use of military force in Iraq. Bush also sought and received authorization from NATO, and he assembled a coalition of forty nations, including America's oldest ally, Great Britain, to enforce the Security Council ultimatum. During those ten months, the only important authority that did not come to the conclusion that force was necessary was the Security Council, where China and Russia could exercise their vetoes to frustrate U.S. policy. Despite the impressive breadth of domestic and international consensus on the necessity of an invasion, it took only three months for the Democrats to turn their backs on the war they had authorized and the president who was leading it.

What explains this betrayal? Not the facts on the ground in Iraq or any principles Bush had allegedly violated. Democrats betrayed the troops and turned their backs on the war for one reason and one reason alone: to gain political power at home. At the time of the Democrats' about-face, the Democratic presidential contest was under way, and an antiwar leftist, Howard Dean, was leading the pack. By June, three months into the fighting, Dean was burying supporters of the war among primary voters and was poised to take the nomination. Until then, John Kerry and John Edwards had been full-throated supporters of the use of force in Iraq.

Kerry's October speech on the floor of the Senate in support of the authorization bill explained why the forcible removal of Saddam was necessary
to defend America and secure the peace. But then came Dean's surge in the
polls. When Kerry saw that he was going to lose the party's nomination, he
switched sides, turning his back on everything he had said in defense of the
war.

Kerry and the Democrats betrayed the war they had authorized; they
betrayed the young Americans they had sent into harm's way; they betrayed
the country they had sworn to serve; and they did it to win political power.
No conservative in his right mind would behave like this. No conservative
would regard control of the federal government as the path to a brave new
world that would justify such sedition. No conservative would betray his
country and the young Americans fighting for it for the sake of such a
ridiculous pipe dream.

It didn't really matter what *issues* Democrats cited in their case against
the president and the war in Iraq. The issues were never the issue. *Power*
was the issue. To defend their about-face on the war, the Democrats claimed
that Bush had invaded Iraq over weapons of mass destruction and that he
had lied in saying Saddam had them. This too was false. The Gulf War truce
and the seventeen UN resolutions whose violation had triggered the war
were not about existing stockpiles of nuclear and chemical weapons. They
were about ensuring that Saddam would not acquire such weapons if he
did not already have them. The Democrats claimed that Bush had lied about
such weapons in order to fool them into supporting the war. In fact, this
Democratic claim was the biggest lie of the entire war.

Democrats were not fooled into supporting the war by a devious president. George Tenet, the director of the Central Intelligence Agency, which
filed the intelligence reports about weapons of mass destruction, was
appointed by Clinton. John Kerry and other Democrats sat on the Senate
Intelligence Committee. The Democrats had access to *all* the intelligence
information that Bush did. If Bush had attempted to lie to win their support
for the war, they would have known he was lying or been able to find out

easily that he was. Bush could not have persuaded the Democrats to support the war by lying about the intelligence even if he had wanted to.

Why, then, did the Democrats accuse Bush of lying? Because they could not admit the actual reason that they had betrayed the war and the young men and women they had sent to battle. They betrayed the war and the troops on the battlefield in order to get elected; they sacrificed American interests and American lives for partisan political gain. This was what they could not admit and the reason they had to claim they were duped. Unfortunately, no Republicans had the political courage or sense to hold them accountable, and Americans are now paying the price for that as the Middle East spins out of control.

For the next five years, while the shooting war continued, the Democrats conducted a scorched-earth campaign against their country and its leader. The harm they did was irreparable. They sabotaged the war effort, including the wider war with Islamic jihadists. Because of the political divisions at home, the Bush administration was unable to follow Saddam's weapons and generals into Syria, where they had fled; or to take the war to Iran, which supplied the IEDs that killed most of our soldiers; or to close the Iraqi borders with Syria and Jordan, which jihadists crossed to fight our troops. The Democrats are therefore responsible for the vacuum in the Middle East that the terrorists and the Russians eventually filled.

Once the Democrats recaptured the presidency, events in the Middle East exposed their destructive farce. Unlike the majority of his colleagues, Senator Barack Obama had always opposed the war in Iraq. He was against American interventions in sovereign countries, and he was against presidents who acted unilaterally and in haste. Or so he said. But when Obama became president and had the power to do so, he invaded Libya, a country whose dictator had closed down his nuclear and chemical weapons programs and that posed no conceivable threat to the United States. Obama intervened unilaterally and without authorization. And he lied about the cause. He claimed he had intervened to prevent civilian massacres, but no evidence supported the claim. He claimed he was intervening to protect human rights, but the intervention had the opposite result. In the ensuing chaos, al Qaeda enjoyed a resurgence and the people of Libya found themselves in a worse state than before.[27]

Obama's invasion of Libya was not merely unilateral; it was egomaniacal. He consulted no one outside his White House inner circle—not his own party, not the Congress, and not the United Nations. Unlike Bush, he acted without constitutional authority and he acted alone. Yet not one Democratic leader opposed him; not one stood up for the principles they had all invoked to cripple America's war in Iraq. Not a single Democratic leader criticized his aggression. Democrats abandoned the principles of multilateralism, consultation with Congress, and international sanction. Adherence to those principles would have jeopardized *their* power, which is the only consideration that moves them on issues critical to the nation's security.

The differences between conservatives and progressives have consequences that are profound. They put our nation at risk. And the most important battle in the world today is not being waged in the Middle East but here at home, in the United States.

CHAPTER FOUR

FIGHT FIRE WITH FIRE

In the years following my departure from the Left, I often reflected on the damage the sixties had inflicted on our country, and our leaders' flaccid opposition to this destructive force. Where was the "ruling class," I wondered, when those attacks were taking place? Why did the leaders of our educational and political institutions acquiesce in and even abet the often-criminal challenges to the status quo? Why did they fail to enforce their own rules and laws? Why, for example, were student protesters not expelled from the schools they desecrated and tried to shut down? Why were they given platforms to advance their agenda instead?

As the years went on and this subversive Left first infiltrated and then came to dominate the Democratic Party, I found myself asking, Where *is* the ruling class? Why don't they see the threat this radicalized party is posing to their interests and the nation's? Why aren't they mobilizing against such a threat to the free-market system and the very foundations of our democracy? But these questions, it turned out, merely reflected my lingering attachment to Marxist illusions. There is no "ruling class," no unified party of the corporate rich, no establishment organized to defend the status quo. America is a pluralistic society with diverse constituencies and competing centers of power, as it has always been. Ironically, the preponderance of wealth deployed for political agendas is, in fact, squarely aligned with the subversive Left and has been for decades.[1] Progressive policy advocates in the form of tax-exempt foundations control more than *ten times* the resources of their conservative counterparts, investing them in organizations and causes that are anti-capitalist and anti–individual freedom.

The idea that there is a "ruling class" and that conservatism is a movement to defend its privilege is simply a fiction useful to those working to undermine the social order. In fact, the movers of radical transformations have also—and always—been drawn from the ranks of the upper classes. The French Revolution was initiated by French aristocrats, Karl Marx was funded and promoted by a capitalist factory owner, and the Obama socialists are swimming in wealth up to their eyeballs. Money makes one powerful, but it doesn't make one conservative. Just ask the billionaires that George Soros has enlisted in the progressive cause.[2]

If the unhappy years of Obama's rule have taught us anything, it is this: *elections have consequences.* The electoral triumphs of the Left have already had a devastating impact on the nation and its future. America is now a world power in decline, a bystander in international events where it was once able to shape them. Its commander in chief actively encourages our enemies and weakens our friends and has steadily diminished our military strength. Domestically, Obama's policies have propelled us toward bankruptcy and constitutional disorder and worse. If a governing party possesses the kind of information about individual lives that the federal government is already accumulating, and if that party is willing to use it politically, it can destroy any opponent and impose its will by executive order. Opposing the Obama Democrats is no longer a matter of curtailing government spending and lowering tax rates. It is a matter of defending the freedom of every American against the advancing powers of a despotic state.

In the 2012 election cycle, Mitt Romney had a good message and an obvious one: *Obama's economic recovery is a sorry failure; twenty-three million people are still jobless; many more are underemployed; if you want jobs and economic opportunities, support the job creators and innovators and deregulators, not those who are attacking them.* This message should have worked. But a critical majority of the voting public never heard it. The reason? A $200 million television ad campaign[3] successfully smeared the messenger as a heartless job destroyer, a mouthpiece of the selfish rich, and a person one couldn't trust.

What was the response of the Romney campaign and the conservative PACs to this killer attack? They didn't have one. There was no $200 million campaign exposing Obama's lies, destroying *his* credibility, and undermining *his* message. Obama's opponents never laid a glove on his character and failed to neutralize his attacks.

Would it have been difficult to do so? Obama is undoubtedly the most obvious and determined liar in presidential history. He is an absentee executive, notably missing in crisis after crisis or busy complaining he was uninformed about matters of crucial concern. While Egypt and Syria burned, he golfed and attended campaign fund-raising events. His endless dithering, misguided interventions, and steadfast support of the Muslim Brotherhood helped to set the Middle East aflame. Meanwhile, he and his wife carry on like royalty, consuming tens of millions of taxpayer dollars on their family vacations and dog, while tens of millions of Americans suffer historic levels of deprivation because of his policies.

How is it possible that his opponents were unable to bury him under his own disasters? Why did two successive Republican opponents, McCain and Romney, characterize this selfish, irresponsible purveyor of false hopes as a "good man"—someone who only lacked experience for the job? How about a moral conscience?

The answer to these questions is obvious but not easily mentioned in public. No one would confront Obama the way he deserved to be confronted, because he is *black*. Actually, Obama is half-black, raised by whites and one Indonesian—but no matter, since racist liberals have made the color of a person's skin decisive. Because Obama is a man "of color," no political figure will hold him to the standard to which others are held or confront him with his failures. Every Republican political consultant will advise that this can't be done. That is how race conscious and prejudiced America has become under the influence of progressive ideas.

Obama's multiple lies about his signature healthcare legislation eventually did damage his credibility. But he was still able to remain remarkably unaccountable, particularly in light of the many scandals in which he was clearly enmeshed that would have brought other politicians down. When all is said and done, this racial Teflon is the reason Republicans lose elections. For what is true of Obama is true of the Democratic Party and progressives generally. They succeed in presenting themselves as the defenders of minorities, whom they use as human shields to protect their own vulnerabilities while they go on the offensive and portray their critics as racists. If conservatives are unable to repel and neutralize these squalid Democratic attacks, they can't hold Democrats accountable. They can't hold Obama accountable, and by extension they can't hold any progressive accountable. Because this is how they fight.

The Left's campaign narrative is always the same: *We are the defenders of the underdog, the advocates of equality and fairness. If you attack us, you are really attacking minorities, women, children, and the poor. If you oppose us, you are racists—the people who supported segregation and lynching.* If anyone thinks this is far-fetched, consider that Kathleen Sebelius, Obama's secretary of Health and Human Services, said exactly this about opponents of Obamacare, glossing over the fact that segregation, like slavery, was once a plank in the Democratic Party platform.[4]

Any effective counterstrategy to these Democratic offensives must take the form of an attack. The attack must expose the Democrats' hypocrisy, tarring their character in the same way and to the same degree that current Democratic attacks taint conservatives'. It must pack the emotional wallop that will neutralize the assaults.

The first question in devising such a strategy should be, how is it possible that Democrats and progressives can pose as defenders of minorities and the poor? For generations, Democrats have controlled the cities of Detroit, Chicago, Cincinnati, Philadelphia, Minneapolis, St. Louis, Washington, D.C., and dozens of other urban blight zones. The number of African American lives damaged or destroyed in these cities by Democrats would exceed the wildest dreams of any Klansman. The administration of Barack Obama is directly responsible for more poverty than any administration since Jimmy Carter's. In the fifth year of Obama's rule, forty-seven million Americans were on food stamps and a hundred million were receiving government handouts, while ninety-three million Americans of working age had given up on finding a job and left the work force. "The data is going to indicate," PBS's Tavis Smiley admitted in a candid moment, "sadly, that when the Obama administration is over, black people will have lost ground in every single leading economic indicator category."[5] Yet every four years—and in between—Democrats are able to persuade people that *they* are defenders of minorities and the poor.

How do they do it? Obviously not by helping minorities and the poor, except to throw them scraps from the government table. They do it by attacking conservatives and the rich as uncaring and oppressive. They portray conservatives as the enemies of minorities and the poor, and rich people as refusing to pay their fair share. They portray their political opponents as *racist*. By demonizing conservatives and demonizing wealth, they are able to pretend they are friends of minorities and the poor, even as they leave them mired in dependency and exploit them for political gain.

Conservatives habitually fail to appreciate the cynicism of these attacks. Democrats don't actually hate rich people or believe they are oppressors. Democratic Party socialists *want* to be rich. In fact, they *are* rich—filthy rich. Just ask George Soros, Jon Corzine, Nancy Pelosi, Rahm Emanuel, Terry McAuliffe, Bill Clinton, and the White House couple who aspire to join them in the economic empyrean. As far as progressives are concerned, rich people are fine if—but only if—they toe the party line and support its destructive agenda. This may be cynicism on steroids, but it is also a winning strategy. By attacking Republicans as racists, you demonstrate that you are a friend of minorities; by attacking taxpayers as selfish, you show that you are a friend of the poor. Never mind that minorities and the poor are worse off under your rule. Politically, the strategy works.

How can believers in individual rights and free markets expose this charade and repel the attacks? How can they neutralize the slanders and show that it is actually conservatives who defend opportunity and independence for minorities and the poor, for working Americans and the middle class? How can conservatives turn the tables on the Left? It's not rocket science: *Turn their guns around. Fight fire with fire.*

Remind people that in the real world, progressives make the lives of poor and minority Americans worse—much worse. Shove this fact in their faces every time you open your mouth to speak. Here is the mantra: In every inner city, the selfish exploiters of the poor are Democrats, progressives, and so-called liberals, and they have been for fifty to a hundred years. Democrats fatten themselves on the votes of the poor while blocking their opportunities for a better life.

The city of Detroit is a gruesome example of how fifty years of Democratic rule can bring a city down and inflict misery on those who cannot afford to leave it. Today, Detroit is the poorest large city in America, but it was not always so. In 1961, Detroit was actually the richest city in the country, the jewel in industrial America's crown. But that year, a liberal Democrat won the mayoral race and took over the municipal administration. James Cavanaugh launched an era of massive government programs and fifty years of monopoly Democratic rule. He institutionalized liberal attitudes toward criminals by ending stop-and-frisk laws, imposed investment-killing regulations, and exacted burdensome taxes to finance his progressive schemes. A succession of Democratic mayors moved these programs and attitudes steadily left. The most important among them was Coleman Young, a progressive Democrat, a secret member of the Communist Party, and an infamous race baiter whose policies during a destructive twenty-year reign sent nonblacks scurrying to the suburbs, taking their tax revenues with them. Fifty years after the Democrats began their rampage, Detroit's taxes were the highest among the fifty largest cities, while its property values ranked last. Both were direct consequences of the city's wars on property and wealth.[6]

By 2011, after five decades of Democratic rule, nearly half Detroit's population was either unemployed or no longer looking for work. Its poverty rate was 36 percent—more than twice that of Michigan as a whole. Over a third of its inhabitants were on food stamps. Its median household income was $28,000—roughly *half* the median income of the citizens of Michigan or the United States. The city employed thirteen thousand municipal workers, one for every fifty-five inhabitants. Corruption was rampant. Multiple city officials, including Coleman Young's police chief and Mayor Kwame Kilpatrick, went to jail for bribery and related crimes. In 2013 Detroit's government was declared bankrupt with $14 billion in long-term debt, primarily driven by unfunded pension and retirement healthcare obligations, a product of the collusion between left-wing government officials and left-wing government unions.[7]

One result of this experiment in progressive rule was an unprecedented flight of Detroit's inhabitants. In 1960, just before the Democrats took over, Detroit was the fourth-largest city in America, with a population of nearly two million. Today fully two-thirds of that population is gone, and the future of those who stayed is bleak.[8] Three out of four children in Detroit are born out of wedlock. Statistically speaking, a child raised in a single-parent, female-headed household is five times more likely to be poor than a child raised in a two-parent family regardless of race or other circumstance.[9] If the first rung on the ladder of success is growing up in an intact family, the second rung is education, and progressives have destroyed that too. A third of Detroit's children don't graduate high school, while nearly half of those who do are functionally illiterate and will never qualify for a decent job.[10]

In one generation, progressives and Democrats reduced America's number one industrial city to the level of a third-world nation. Because 82 percent of its present population is African American, Detroit is a showcase of the damage Democrats have done to this minority group. If conservatives spoke the same language as Democrats, they would be calling the devastation of Detroit the most appalling racial atrocity since segregation. But Republicans don't even mention Detroit. Not a single notable campaign speech or ad in the 2012 campaign featured the plight of Detroit's African American population.

To one degree or another, Detroit's nightmare is repeated in Democratic-run cities across the nation. It is a fact that the government of virtually every major city in America is 100 percent controlled by Democrats and has been for decades—for over a hundred years in some cities, such as Milwaukee and El Paso. Everything wrong with America's inner cities that can be attributed to policy is the Democrats' responsibility. They have their boot on the necks of poor black and Hispanic families. But Republicans are mute.

Democrats don't care about the devastating impact of their policies on minorities and the poor. They derive such electoral and monetary benefits from their inner-city plantations that they will fight anyone who dares to challenge them. In 2003, the businessman and philanthropist Robert Thompson offered $200 million to Detroit to open fifteen new charter high schools.[11] But Thompson was forced to withdraw his proposal after it drew angry criticism from the city's teacher union, which argued (falsely) that the charter schools would drain millions of dollars from public schools.

Democrats' dedication to failure was on display even more dramatically in the nation's capital when Adrian Fenty became mayor, in 2007. In no city in this country is the crime committed by Democrats and their union supporters against African American children more outrageous than in Washington, D.C. The city has been run exclusively by Democrats for half a century, and its schools are among the lowest performing in the country. It is no mystery why inner-city schools like Washington's are failing. Teachers have lifetime jobs, and there is no connection between their performance and their rewards. Good teachers and bad teachers are paid the same. They get automatic pay raises for showing up and can't be fired no matter how incompetent they are. Teachers' unions and Democrats blame the failure of these schools on overcrowded classrooms and lack of money. But when Fenty became mayor, Washington's classrooms had a teacher-to-student ratio of one to twelve,[12] and taxpayers provided more than $29,000 to educate each child.[13] That is equivalent to tuition for the most elite private schools in the country. Washington's children ought to have been getting the best education money could buy. And yet the story of the capital city's public schools was one of abject failure for its African American children.

By any measure Adrian Fenty was an extraordinary political talent when he entered the Democratic mayoral primary in 2006. His opponent was the chairman of the city council, with twenty-five years of experience in city government and an endorsement by the popular retiring mayor. Despite these odds, Fenty won the primary by 26 points, carrying all 142 precincts—an unprecedented feat. He then won the general election with 89 percent of the vote.

It is safe to say that this young man—he was all of thirty-six at the time—had a bright political future and would one day be a national figure. But Adrian Fenty cared about one thing more than his political career. He cared about those children. He got legislation passed that put him personally in charge of the schools and made educational reform his priority. He hired Michelle Rhee, an education reformer, as the new school chancellor. He closed dangerous and underused schools and laid off incompetent teachers. When there was a budget shortfall, the city council recommended that he cut summer school for kids who needed remedial training. Instead, Fenty came up with the money by firing a raft of underperforming teachers. He successfully waged a two-year battle for a new union contract, which ended lifetime tenure and connected teacher performance to reward. Michelle Rhee fired 241 incompetent teachers and put another 737 on notice that they had been rated "minimally effective."[14]

The results were dramatic. At Sousa Middle School, in one of the district's most impoverished neighborhoods, 84 percent of the students had math and reading scores below the minimal standards when Fenty and Rhee took charge. In other words they were functionally illiterate. In just one year of the Fenty-Rhee reform administration, students at Sousa posted substantial gains in reading and math proficiency, meeting the federal benchmarks for progress for the first time in the school's history. Graduation rates for D.C. schools increased every year, and SAT scores improved by 72 percent. And it was not just the schools that Mayor Fenty improved. Economic development flourished, and violent crime registered a double-digit decline.

But another mayoral election soon loomed, and Adrian Fenty was about to lose it. The unions and the Left united behind a Democratic primary challenger to defeat Fenty and run him out of town and out of politics for good. He was defeated for the same the reason that the schools had been a failure. Public schools in America's inner cities are not there for the children but as jobs programs for adults and slush funds for the Democratic Party and its union allies. The adults are organized and the children are not. So in a Democratic primary in a Democratic city where he had stepped out of line, Adrian Fenty had to face the wrath and resources of the government unions and the demagogic politicians they own. The party supported a primary challenger, and the head of the AFL-CIO himself came into town to campaign against Fenty and seal his defeat.

Some Republicans complain that Democrats win because they hand out goodies. They certainly do. But the goodies they hand out are nothing compared with what they've destroyed for all Americans and particularly for minorities and the poor. How many people, given the choice, would rather live on handouts than have a job that allows them to stand on their own two feet and pay for what they need and want? Not that many. Not enough to defeat Republicans if they would attack their opponents, aggressively and remorselessly, for the devastation they have inflicted on the poor and the working class.

It is a cliché that the best defense is a good offense, but that's because it is true. The winning strategy is this: Attack the Democrats and progressives for their war against minorities and the poor. Use the same morally infused language that they do. Expose their empty promises and their hypocrisy.

Subvert their message by focusing relentlessly on their betrayal of the very people they pretend to support. In attacking Democrats as enemies of minorities and the poor, conservatives will show that they care what happens to minorities and the poor. This will put the Democrats on the defensive and neutralize their malicious attacks.

Going on offense has another advantage: well-placed attacks change the story line. Republicans had planned to make the 2012 election about Obamacare because of that issue's potency in the 2010 midterm election, which produced a Republican landslide. But two things happened on the way to the election that changed the subject. First, Romney's selection of Paul Ryan as his running mate gave Democrats an easy target—Ryan's comprehensive budget plan—and enabled them to neutralize and divert the Republican attack. Second, and far more important, a movement called Occupy Wall Street rampaged through American cities attacking the so-called 1 percent and the allegedly unfair distribution of wealth. Occupy Wall Street was a criminal mob organized and financed by Democrat-connected government unions and supported by Obama.[15] Overnight, the mayhem caused by the Occupiers changed the national subject from health plans to "fairness." They cast anyone opposing more taxes as a selfish defender of the rich, putting Republicans on the defensive and taking Obamacare off the radar.

One of the Democrats' most effective charges in the 2012 campaign was that Republicans were waging a "war on women" because they didn't want to finance contraceptives for upper-middle-class academic females like Sandra Fluke. The answer to this attack is not to argue about contraceptives, which will lose a lot of single women's votes. The answer is this: After a full term of Obama, there are sixteen million women on food stamps. Two out of five single mothers are on food stamps. Under Obamacare, family healthcare costs are about to skyrocket. This is Obama's war on women. It has to be stopped.

Democrats accuse Republicans of being anti-Hispanic. After five years of Obama, there are eight million Hispanics on food stamps, and twenty million Hispanics are unemployed or no longer looking for work. Family healthcare costs under Obamacare are about to skyrocket. This is Obama's war on Hispanics. It has to be stopped.

Democrats accuse Republicans of not caring about blacks. Look at America's inner cities. America's inner cities have been run by Democrats for fifty years. This is their war on African Americans and the poor. It has to be stopped.

It's not rocket science. It's about turning the guns around. It's about having the moral fiber to do it.

Going negative is important, but elections cannot be won by going negative alone. Going negative is necessary to put opponents on the defensive and blunt their attacks. But people also need hope, and they are looking for change; these elements are basic components of any campaign. In a political message, the positives should highlight the negatives. Positive proposals should spotlight the way progressive policies specifically hurt minorities, working Americans, and the poor. In opposing those who oppress and exploit these people, Republicans will demonstrate they care about what happens to the powerless and the vulnerable. It's a simple equation, but Republicans somehow don't get it.

For an obvious example of how Republicans can communicate a positive message while at the same time hitting Democrats where they're vulnerable, consider education. Let's take the money that taxpayers hand over to bureaucrats who don't care about the children in failing schools and give it back to families who do care. Let's give vouchers to *every* student in America and undercut the bureaucracies that have put students last. Instead of calling for the abolition of the Department of Education, let's call for a fundamental change in its mission. Let's spend its $50 billion budget on the administration of a scholarship program for all Americans from kindergarten through college. Let's put those education dollars in the hands of every poor and middle-class person in America. Let's launch this effort with a $100 million television ad campaign to tell Americans how progressives in every major urban school system have destroyed the lives of poor children, mainly black and Hispanic, who can't afford the private schools where those same progressives send their own children. We might remind them that Barack and Michelle Obama send their own daughters to Washington's ultra-exclusive Sidwell Friends School (annual tuition: $35,000 per child). And that's par for the course for Democrats who oppose school choice.

Let's put hope in the hands of people who can't afford to send their kids to schools that will teach them. Let's change the way the educational economy works, so that individuals are empowered, not government bureaucrats. Let's change the system so that competition is restored and standards are raised. Let's take the second-biggest part of the government economy and return it to the people. Let's create a model of the kind of society we want—a society that features free markets and is based on individual achievement, not government-defined collectives.

This is a suggestion for one possible campaign. Even if it doesn't win on the first or second offering, it will still change the perceptions of everyone in politics. Conservatives will no longer be seen as defenders of the rich but as defenders of principles and policies that benefit minorities and the poor, along with everyone else. And progressives will be seen as oppressors. If campaigns like this are conducted correctly, they will change not only the way conservatives frame their message but the political landscape and the prospects for the nation's future.

CHAPTER FIVE

UNITING THE RIGHT

Anyone paying attention to politics soon notices that when Democrats attack, they speak from the same text, and when they march to the polls, they march in lockstep. If one Democrat says the wealthy must pay their "fair share," all Democrats say it—regardless of the merits of the charge. If their leaders say Republicans want to shut down the government in order to deny Americans affordable healthcare, the rest will follow—no matter how far-fetched the claim. When a cornerstone program like Obamacare is being put in place, not only do Democrats get behind it as one, every player on the political Left—journalists, professors, talk-show hosts, union heads, MoveOn radicals, and Occupy anarchists—falls into line and promotes it with identical words. They act in "solidarity" in fair political weather and foul, and they do it even for programs like Obamacare, which was ill conceived, deceptively presented, and self-evidently fiscally unsound. When the Democratic voices all come together, the amplification is stupefying.

The result: a morally bankrupt, politically tyrannical, economically destructive party is able to put an entire nation on the road to disaster.

By contrast, Republicans speak with multiple voices using words that often are unrelated. If one Republican leader says, "Don't intervene in Syria," another says, "Don't hesitate." If one says, "Obama-supported immigration reform will be a dagger aimed at American sovereignty," another says, "Opposition to immigration reform will sound a death knell for our party." If one Republican leader says, "Defund Obamacare," others say, "Fund the government," even if that might mean funding Obamacare. These contending voices are multiplied by conservative talking heads in the media who march to their own political drummers. The result is a cacophony of voices, which in the end point nowhere. Because Republicans speak with many voices, their message is diluted, hard to hear, and difficult to understand.

Internal dissension not only blunts Republican attacks, it hands Democrats a convenient stick to beat them with. No one on the Right thinks this is an advantageous situation. Why, then, is it the case? What force that unites Democrats do Republicans lack? The missing factor cannot be a party whip enforcing discipline, since both have them. Moreover, there are no whips to rein in factions outside legislatures, whether grassroots supporters or media voices who often command larger audiences than the elected officials themselves. But that also goes for both sides. Like Republicans, Democrats lack a formal mechanism to bring their media sympathizers and allies in line. So how do they do it? How do they close their ranks as they go into battle?

What Democrats have that Republicans lack is the power of a unifying idea. A unifying idea is not a consensus about policy or an agreement about tactics. Unanimity in such matters is difficult to achieve and impossible to sustain. People on the Left are often fractious when it comes to specific policies and tactics. Their unity is inspired—*forged* is a better word—by a missionary idea. On the eve of his election in 2008, Barack Obama said to his followers, "We are five days away from fundamentally transforming the United States of America."[1] That idea—the idea of changing the entire framework of the nation's life, of making "a better world"—is what unites the Left and gives it power.

No conservative thinks or talks like this. But progressives do. It is what makes them progressives. Belief in a better world achieved by their efforts is their identity in the same way "Christian" and "Jew" are the identities of people with those religious faiths. The vision of a fundamentally transformed society is what creates their unity and inspires them to march in lockstep.

HOW THE IDEA WORKS

"Progressive," "socialist," and "liberal" are today interchangeable terms that describe participants in a moral crusade with a political agenda, usually referred to as "social justice." It can be summed up as equality imposed by the state. The quest for a utopia of equals forges progressive alliances, defines their allegiances, and justifies the means they are willing to use to get there. They may differ on policies and tactics to advance the cause. But they are ever ready to subordinate their differences to achieve the common goal. Since the Democratic Party has become a party of the Left, progressive missionaries view it as the practical vehicle for making their idea a reality. They are willing to follow its marching orders because a political party that controls the state is the only way to achieve the goal.

The reasoning behind this behavior was succinctly summarized in a statement made by the Russian revolutionary Leon Trotsky, explaining why he would not leave the Bolshevik Party even after Stalin, his archenemy and eventual executioner, became its absolute leader. Trotsky said, "We can only be right with and by the Party, for history has provided no other way of being in the right…. If the Party adopts a decision which one or other of us thinks unjust, he will say, just or unjust, it is my party, and I shall support the consequences of the decision to the end."[2]

Non-Bolsheviks may not share Trotsky's metaphysical certitude, but they will recognize the political principle. If the mission is to change the world and there is only one party with the will and means to do it, even though it might be wrong on this or that matter, its fortunes must be advanced and its power defended. The commitment is even more intense when the opposition party is viewed as an enemy of the cause. If Republicans are seen as the party of privilege at war with minorities, women, and the poor, then their ideas are not only wrong but evil. If someone does not side with the angels to fight injustice, that person can be considered of the devil's party, which is how progressives normally view Republicans. "One acts decisively," Saul Alinsky writes in *Rules for Radicals*, "only in the conviction that all of the angels are on one side and the devils are on the other."[3]

Religious conviction is a powerful unifier. The verbal assaults that demonize opponents inspire two related fears: (1) Fear of being politically incorrect; and (2) Fear of joining the ranks of the damned. Both help to keep the faithful in line and assure they will speak with a single voice.

"Our enemies [are] always immoral," writes Alinsky. For progressives, the political issue is never the issue. The issue is always the immorality of those who oppose the progressive idea—conservatives and Republicans. They are damned not because of what they say, but because of who they are and what they stand for. Since the conservative outlook is immoral, the policies conservatives advocate are not to be trusted, and their arguments must be dismissed. Because progressives regard politics as a battle between light and darkness (I have heard Democratic legislators actually invoke this comparison), they are less concerned about which policies will work than what will help their party to win. Politics, for them, is a conflict between good and evil, between the party of "progress" and the party of "reaction." This dichotomy decides most questions in advance of their consideration. Progressives have a saying that expresses their attitude: "We are on the right side of history, and Republicans are on the wrong side."[4] What more need be said?

When he became president, Obama had a carpet placed in the Oval Office into which was woven the progressive sentiment, "The moral arc of the universe is long, but it bends towards justice."[5] *Their* justice; *their* cause. The issue is never the issue. The issue is always what will bring power to those who have taken up the progressive cause and help them to bring the future closer. It is not a particular policy or tactic that matters in the end; what matters is the cause.

The right is an extremely diverse coalition. It does have a unifying idea but rarely articulates it and does not attempt to rally its forces behind it. In general, therefore, conservatives do not speak from the same page or march in political lockstep; their divisions are bared for all to see and for their opponents to exploit. Conservative media are frequently at odds with the Republican Party, and the Republican Party is often at odds with itself. An entire movement has emerged in the "Tea Parties" because of rank-and-file dissatisfaction with the way Republicans conduct themselves in conflicts with their Democratic opponents. To be sure, there is also a progressive grassroots that has significant disagreements with the Democratic Party. But when it comes to elections, to deciding who will get the power, the progressive grassroots falls into line. It does so for the good of the cause, to be on the right side of history.

By way of contrast, conservatives are not averse to sitting on their hands at election time or even voting for the other camp. Why do conservatives do this? Because they think elections are about specific policies, and they often don't see the larger cause. This myopia develops because Republicans do not frame their campaigns as moral crusades and do not mobilize their troops under the banner of a morally uplifting, unifying idea. Instead, their focus is on particular policies and tactical issues, which divide their followers, promote divisions in their ranks, and frequently put them at odds with their political base.

If policy and tactics were Democrats' primary concerns, they too would be divided. Their united support of the unpopular healthcare bill is a prime example of what happens when a policy is regarded as a pillar of the transformational cause. The troops bury their doubts and are willing to close ranks because they understand this measure is a cornerstone of the progressive dream. Republicans were uncharacteristically unified in their opposition to the bill because the Democrats permitted no compromise and sought no Republican contribution to the plan. Republicans are unified only when Democrats give them no option to be otherwise. If Republicans and conservatives continue to approach issues in isolation from each other and fail to formulate a unifying goal, they will eventually lose the war and everything that depends on it.

THE CONSERVATIVE CAUSE

The first reaction of conservatives to this advice will be to reject it. Conservatives do not want to behave like leftists who see politics as a means to change the world. Conservatives don't believe in such transformation and regard those who seek it as misguided at best and more than likely dangerous. Conservatives' caution is temperamental and comes from their view that the source of society's problems is human beings themselves. Consequently, they regard political "solutions" as inevitably flawed and likely to require constant reforms to repair the problems they themselves will create. Conservatives look at the key legislative pillars of the progressive future—Social Security and Medicare—and see that they are already bankrupt. The welfare state has created more—and worse—poverty than it was designed to cure. Why would a massive new entitlement like Obamacare, based on these already-failed "solutions," work any better? That is the question that conservatives ask.

The same conservative skepticism guided the nation's Founders. They understood that democracy can work only through compromise, and they devised measures to encourage it. Progressives pay lip service to this attitude, but they don't really believe in it. There can be no permanent compromise of utopian goals like social justice and equality, no lasting *modus vivendi* with those who oppose human progress.

As the tragic history of the twentieth century shows, the progressive cause is ultimately a war on human nature and therefore a war on individual freedom. The powerful progressive challenge Americans now face is a call to arms for conservatives. Conservatism is by nature a defensive posture. It is about protecting the constitutional framework of checks and balances to thwart transformative schemes. When challenged, a defense becomes a positive cause, and the creation of this constitutional framework was itself a revolutionary act. The Founders created a political system to limit government and maximize freedom because their own freedom was under attack. Conservatism is about individual freedom, which is its natural, unifying idea.

Individual freedom is based on rights that are independent of the political process. Government, therefore, must be limited. That is the inspirational idea that unites the political Right, and it is an idea that is fundamentally opposed to "equality" as progressives and Democrats define it. The equality proclaimed in the Declaration of Independence is not an equality of abilities and is therefore not denied by disparities in results, which is the equality that progressives seek. The equality of the Founders—the only equality compatible with individual freedom—is equality of opportunity, reflecting the equal status that individuals enjoy in the eyes of their Creator. It is an equality of individuals—not as men or women, whites or blacks, but as immortal souls. That is the way the Founders conceived equality and why they believed that every individual, however unequal, must be regarded with equal respect in the eyes of the law.

The equality demanded by progressives and Democrats is not just a distraction from the equality the Founders proclaimed. It can be achieved—if at all—only by a war on individual freedom. In devising the constitutional arrangements that created the Republic, the Founders' express purpose was to thwart the progressive ambitions of the day, which included "a rage for paper money, for an abolition of debts, for an equal division of property, or for any other improper or wicked project."[6] Liberty and equality of results are inevitably in conflict. Because of the unequal distribution of talents, abilities, and virtues, freedom can exist only when these inequalities, which James Madison called a "diversity of faculties," are protected. This diversity is the source, as Madison further observed, "from which property rights originate," and "the protection of these faculties is the first object of government."[7] In other words, government should protect the *inequalities* that arise from the diversity of natural abilities, talents, and character, and thus protect the right of its citizens to pursue their individual happiness.

This fact of human nature stands in the way of the progressive schemers. It is the cause of the division of Americans into conservatives and progressives, defenders of liberty and its would-be destroyers. The steady erosion of freedom in the last half century is the direct consequence of progressives' political advances. The progressive agenda is a systematic assault on the private sector, which is precisely the realm of individual freedom. The goal of each progressive program is the subordination of the private sector to the power of the state. Conservatives need to recognize that there is a war going on; and they need to wage it properly as a defense of freedom. *This* is the unifying idea of the conservative cause.

Republicans should frame their policies and tactical positions in terms of this unifying idea. Economic redistribution is not "fairness," as progressives maintain. It is theft and therefore a war on freedom. Compulsory public schools are not a service to minorities and the poor but infringements on their freedom to choose a good education and pursue the American dream. Obamacare mandates not only drive up costs and diminish the quality of care, they infringe on choice—the freedom of individuals to manage their own healthcare as they think best. Massive government deficits are not accounting problems; they are a war on the ability of individuals to work for themselves instead of the government and are therefore an attack on the pursuit of happiness. This is the moral language with which Republicans need to indict their opponents—the true enemies of social justice and social fairness. It is the cause that will unify the conservative base and rally those who remain committed to the (classically) liberal values of the American Founding.

During the Cold War with the Communist bloc, the cause of freedom provided Republicans with national majorities. Since the 1988 presidential contest, the last before the Communist collapse, Republicans have won a majority of the popular vote in only one national election. Republican victories during the Cold War demonstrate how powerful the unifying idea of freedom was when Republicans rallied behind it. During the Cold War, national security provided the key to Republican victories because it framed their cause as a crusade for freedom.

The defense of America is a defense of the idea of individual freedom. That is why the Left is not particularly happy with national security issues and why it consistently seeks to diminish America's military strength. For the first time in our modern history, attacks on America's world role are supported by a sizeable portion of our own population, including the president himself. Unfortunately, Republicans have been slow to recognize the threat and have failed to frame the national security issue in a way that confronts the uncertain loyalties of the Left and its unsteady commitment to the nation's cause. We now face a new totalitarian enemy in political Islam, led by the Muslim Brotherhood and the fascist regimes in Syria and Iran. Without attempting to remake the world, Republicans need to support and strengthen America's role as a defender of freedom, beginning with its own.

The struggle that inspired conservatives in the Cold War era—the battle between tyranny and freedom—is once again on America's doorstep. But Republicans are reluctant to name it. The Republican silence on national security must end. It is time to connect the struggles for individual freedom at home and the defense of our free society abroad, and to make them one. That is the sure way to advance the Republican message and to unify the political forces on which the future of our nation depends.

DESTRUCTIVE SOCIAL JUSTICE
(WITH JOHN PERAZZO)

n a cynical gesture to secure his reelection in 1996, Bill Clinton declared that "the era of big government is over."[1] Fifteen years later, on the eve of Barack Obama's reelection, the same Bill Clinton published a big-government manifesto, hailing it as the key to a caring and prosperous America.[2] This was also a campaign ploy, part of a massive effort by progressives to justify Obama's multitrillion-dollar spending spree and promote his reelection.[3] Ignoring the anemic results of Obama's "stimulus" programs for everyone except his political cronies and campaign bundlers, progressives argued that an even greater expansion of the state was required for a "strong economy" and a "fair" society. Only social reactionaries and the willfully blind would deny it.

Ever since the New Deal, Democrats have tried to solve America's social problems with ever more-capacious government troughs. So dedicated are they to social bailouts that their vision is now indistinguishable from the socialism that has brought Europe to the brink of economic ruin. Why does the belief in big government take on the character of a religious faith among political progressives? Because progressives want to change the world and reshape it to conform to their prejudices and desires.

In progressive eyes there are "two Americas": the America of the rich and powerful and the America of the poor and powerless. As they see it, only an ever-expansive, ever more-powerful state can solve the problem of two Americas. An extreme—not to say absurd—version of the "two Americas" trope was the fantasy cooked up by the Occupy Wall Street radicals for the 2012 presidential election, pitting 1 percent of the population against the remaining 99 percent. Not coincidently, Occupy Wall Street was created and funded by Obama-supporting government unions.[4] In the words of the Clinton manifesto, Republican voters are in the grips of "anti-government obsessions" that threaten the nation's prosperity and perpetuate its pressing social problems.[5] The poor and the powerless are ultimately the victims of conservative selfishness.

This is the melodrama the Left plays out in every election cycle. Even though conservatives are actually more generous in their charitable giving than "liberals," they respond to this progressive attack in the manner of nervous accountants attempting to balance a ledger.[6] Talking about "debts" and "deficits," conservatives dodge the moral question instead of answering it. They retreat into numbers as though they don't want to look at the human toll of socialist policies. They wag their fingers at government corruption and waste as though that were all that mattered.

For their part, progressives never stray from the moral indictment, which will always trump a business case. Perhaps it is true that a particular government program is as wasteful as conservatives claim; that's just the price of helping the helpless. Government investments that turn out to be wrong or wasteful are wrong for the right reasons. Shouldn't help be given where help is needed, even if the help sometimes falls short or misses the mark? Isn't erring on the side of compassion and hope better than a heartless addiction to the bottom line? Aren't conservatives responding to social crises by blaming the victims?

To be fair, conservatives also have a human victim to champion, namely the taxpayer. But this victim only provides fodder for the progressive assault. When conservatives wring their hands over taxpayers' woes, they are merely demonstrating that their real concern is to defend the selfish. Why shouldn't the "1 percent" pay a little extra for worthy causes? Why wouldn't they want to share their good fortune with others? Those who defend the selfishness of wealthy taxpayers are enemies of education and welfare, of minorities and the poor. Conservatives are waging a war against society's weak and vulnerable members.

It is *this* issue—the welfare of others and especially the weak and vulnerable—that conservatives have to begin to address if they are to hold their own in the political debate. To make a strong case for limited government and individual freedom, conservatives need to address the concern that Americans have for the well-being of others. They must speak to Americans' hearts and not just their pocketbooks.

This is the argument that conservatives should make: The sins of government are not merely sins of omission; they are also sins of commission. Government programs are not only inadequately conceived and poorly managed—most people will concede as much—but they have destructive consequences for the very people they are designed to help. In other words, government programs have victims too, and those victims are not merely taxpayers. Here are four examples of how government in the hands of progressive politicians has blighted the lives of society's most vulnerable populations, particularly those who are poor and black, and how acts of progressive compassion have inflicted damage on minorities on a scale that can hardly be imagined.

HOW PROGRESSIVES SOLD HOMES TO THE POOR THEY COULDN'T AFFORD AND TOOK BILLIONS IN WEALTH FROM BLACK AND HISPANIC HOMEOWNERS

An almost invisible aspect of the economic crisis of 2008 was its devastating impact on minority households. As a result of the government-fostered collapse of the housing market, the median net worth of black and Hispanic Americans declined by 53 percent and 66 percent, respectively, between 2005 and 2009. This was the single greatest economic blow ever delivered to these communities.[7] Its indisputable origins lie in actions by progressives in the Democratic Party, which in the 1970s began a campaign to make home ownership a right—as a matter of "social justice."

To secure this right, left-wing activists and their Democratic allies accused the banking industry of red-lining minority communities and denying them loans on the basis of race. In forcing banks to rectify the racial disparities in the loans they provided, the social reformers systematically undermined and then destroyed the prudent and financially sound lending standards arrived at through years of experience. The destruction of these standards led directly to the collapse of the housing market in 2008.

There was in fact no systemic racism in the lending industry when progressives and Democrats began their campaign, and there were no insurmountable obstacles to minorities' seeking homes they could actually afford. But facts were unimportant to the Left, which had succeeded in establishing statistical "disparities" as evidence of racism in order to achieve its progressive goals. Statistics did show that home-ownership rates for African Americans and Hispanics, which were slightly above 40 percent, were well below the rate for whites, which was near 70 percent.[8] But many factors are involved in securing a loan to buy a house, and this statistic was not in itself evidence of actual discrimination. For the Left and the Democratic politicians who joined their crusade, however, no further evidence was needed to tar the mortgage industry as racist and strike a blow for social justice.

The congressional point man for the "equal rights in housing" campaign was a McGovern Democrat named Henry Reuss, chairman of the powerful House Banking Committee.[9] Reuss sponsored the Housing and Community Development Act of 1977, a key section of which became known as the Community Reinvestment Act (CRA). The crucial provision of the CRA was the requirement that each federal bank document how it is "helping to meet the credit needs of its entire community, including low- and moderate-income neighborhoods."[10] These records would provide the evidence of racial disparity and become a mandate for banks to seek out minority borrowers of meager to modest means. The argument that the disparity reflected racism was so effective that the Reuss bill passed with 87 percent Republican support and 97 percent Democrat support in the House, and 50 percent Republican support and 87 percent Democrat support in the Senate.[11] It was signed into law by President Carter as a triumph for equal opportunity and civil rights.

Like many government policies, the CRA's mandate expanded once it became law, and it expanded further when the Democrats regained the White House in 1993.[12] The CRA was intended to encourage outreach to minority communities and to ensure that every precaution was taken to prevent discrimination. But officials of the Clinton administration came up with radical interpretations of the law that supported a more aggressive approach. New guidelines were put in place to force banks to abandon previous lending policies and undertake a wholesale restructuring of their lending policies in order to eliminate the racial disparities in the loans they provided.[13] Future president Barack Obama, then a lawyer working with the radical Association of Community Organizations for Reform Now (ACORN), played a leading role in building grassroots support, harassing bank officials, and exerting legal pressure to widen the scope of the CRA mandate and force the banks to comply.[14]

The new standards—if they could be called that—were designed to ensure that large numbers of low-income minorities could qualify for home mortgages even though they had little or no ability to repay the loans. Owning a home would thus become a "right" even for those who could not afford one. The policy made no economic sense, and financial disaster was written all over it. But to point out the dangers or oppose the reform was "racist." Its economic irrationality didn't matter. CRA was justified by the canons of a political religion that sanctified the sale of homes to people who couldn't afford them as a matter of social justice.

To support the campaign to get rid of existing loan standards, the Federal Reserve Bank of Boston published a study in 1992 purporting to show that whites and blacks had been denied mortgages at disparate rates—17 percent for whites and 38 percent for blacks—and attributing the disparity to race.[15] A sympathetic press promoted the report in front-page stories as proof that racism was rampant in the mortgage industry. In the words of the *Boston Globe*, the "landmark study" provided "the most damning evidence to date of racial hurdles facing minority homebuyers."[16]

This conclusion, found in virtually all media accounts, ignored the facts provided in a second study conducted the same year, also by the Boston Federal Reserve Bank. The new study refuted the previous claims. It showed that black loan applicants not only had greater debt burdens and poorer credit histories than their white counterparts, but also tended to seek loans covering a higher percentage of the property values in question.[17] After correcting for these and other standard credit criteria—income, net worth, age, education, and probability of employment—the loan-rejection gap between racial groups all but disappeared.[18] The Federal Reserve Board in Washington also reexamined the original study and found its conclusions "difficult to justify."[19] Nobel Prize–winning economist Gary Becker analyzed the first Boston Fed study and concluded that it had "serious methodological flaws" that made its results "of dubious value in formulating social policy."[20]

Other evidence further discredited the claim of white racism in the banking industry: Asians, for instance, were more likely than whites to be approved for mortgages,[21] and black-owned banks were even more likely than white-owned banks to turn down black applicants.[22] Moreover, black homeowners had higher default rates than whites on their mortgage loans.[23] This was a sure indication that lending institutions were not holding prospective black borrowers to stricter standards in awarding loans but were probably already favoring them.[24]

But even these facts did not deter the Left from indicting the banking industry for allegedly racist practices. Those who challenged the Left's extravagant claims of systemic racism invited the same charge against themselves. Egged on by civil rights groups and an echo-chamber media, the Clinton administration pressed the attack on lending guidelines and the financial system they underpinned. Attorney General Janet Reno warned that "no bank" would be "immune" from the Justice Department's determination to punish alleged discrimination in lending practices—a warning that extended far beyond the subprime loan market.[25] Joining Reno, the comptroller of the currency, Eugene Ludwig, told the Senate Banking Committee, "We have to use every means at our disposal to end discrimination and to end it as quickly as possible."[26]

In this spirit, the administration transformed the CRA from a simple outreach effort into a strict quota system.[27] Under the new arrangements, if a bank failed to meet its quota for loans to low-income minorities, it ran a high risk of failing to earn a "satisfactory" CRA rating from the Federal Deposit Insurance Corporation.[28] Such failure could block a bank's efforts to open a new branch, relocate a home office, make an acquisition, or merge with another financial institution.[29] From a practical standpoint, banks had no recourse but to drastically lower their down payment and underwriting standards and approve risky loans to borrowers who, experience told them, would not be able to pay them back.

Pressure to subvert the normal lending procedures came from radical community organizations such as ACORN and the Greenlining Institute, which were able to intimidate the lending industry by accusing individual banks of discriminatory practices.[30] The accusations of racism were routinely accompanied by threats of lawsuits and boycotts. To forestall the damaging consequences of such actions, banks routinely responded by pledging to increase loans to nonwhites whether or not they had the means to repay them. As a result, banks' CRA commitments grew geometrically to more than thirty times what they had previously been. From 1977 to 1991, subprime loans cumulatively totaled just under $9 billion. In 1992, they jumped to $34 billion. Over the ensuing sixteen years—right to the moment of the housing crash—they expanded to over $6 trillion.[31]

The CRA was by no means the government's only hammer to force financial institutions to "remedy racism" by revising their business practices. In the first year of the Clinton administration, the Department of Housing and Urban Development (HUD) developed rules that pressured lenders to increase their approval rates for loans to minority applicants by 20 percent within a one-year period.[32] HUD also began bringing legal actions against those mortgage bankers who turned down a higher percentage of minority applicants than white applicants, regardless of their reasons for doing so.[33] The only way for lenders to escape punishment was to lower the down-payment requirements to qualify for loans, which eventually went to zero, and to drastically reduce income requirements for minority borrowers.

HUD also pressured the government-sponsored mortgage lenders Fannie Mae and Freddie Mac to earmark a rising number of their loans for low-income borrowers. "For 1996," the *Wall Street Journal* reported, "HUD gave Fannie and Freddie an explicit target: 42 percent of their mortgage financing had to go to borrowers with incomes below the median in their area. By 2005, the target had increased to 52 percent."[34] HUD further required 12 percent of all mortgages purchased by Fannie and Freddie to be "special affordable" loans, typically to borrowers with incomes at least 40 percent below the median for 2008.[35] Nonwhite minorities were far likelier than whites to be the recipients of these loans. In December 2006, the *New York Times* reported, "The most recent Home Mortgage Disclosure Act data from lending institutions show that over half of African Americans and 40 percent of Hispanics received subprime loans."[36]

There was no more-important congressional promoter of the new lending practices than Barney Frank, the ranking Democrat on the powerful House Committee on Financial Services and later its chairman. In 2004, when the mounting danger was clearly visible, Frank dismissed critics' concerns about the high-risk loans. Government, he said, had "probably done too little rather than too much" in pushing Fannie and Freddie "to meet the goals of affordable housing...."[37] Senator Christopher Dodd, the ranking Democrat on the Banking Committee, agreed. As both institutions approached bankruptcy, Dodd referred to Fannie and Freddie as "one of the great success stories of all time." Even as late as 2008, just days before the reckoning, Dodd pronounced them "fundamentally sound and strong."[38]

Democrats were not the only politicians pushing for lax lending standards and justifying them as an effort to benefit minorities and the poor. The specious racism argument prevailed on Republicans too. In 2002, the Bush administration pressed Congress to pass the American Dream Down-payment Initiative (ADDI) to subsidize the down payments of first-time, low-income home buyers.[39] After ADDI was enacted, in 2003, Bush also encouraged Congress to pass legislation permitting the Federal Housing Administration to make zero-down-payment loans at low interest rates to low-income people.[40] The theory was that "those who can afford the monthly payment but have been unable to save for a down-payment should [not] be deprived from owning a home."[41]

In just a few years, the time-tested practices of the entire lending industry had been abandoned under government pressure. One in five mortgages was now financed by a subprime loan, and loans with no money down had risen to nearly 14 percent of all mortgages. But it couldn't go on indefinitely. Like Wile E. Coyote chasing the roadrunner off a cliff, the subprime mortgage business eventually succumbed to the law of gravity, and the vast, rickety subprime structure came crashing down, causing a record number of foreclosures across the United States.[42]

The primary victims of the reckless lending policies were the very people they were supposed to help—the poor and uncreditworthy. Their inability to pay the charges on their loans now cost them their new homes. From January 2007 through the end of 2009, there were 2.5 million housing foreclosures nationwide.[43] Among borrowers who had taken out mortgages in the three years leading up to the 2008 collapse, fully 8 percent of the African Americans and Hispanics lost their homes to foreclosure in the years between 2007 and 2009. Among the less-favored white borrowers, the rate of foreclosure was a little more than half as high.[44] When the Center for Responsible Lending issued a report in June 2010, it estimated that by then 17 percent of Hispanic homeowners and 11 percent of black homeowners (as compared to 7 percent of whites) had already lost their homes or were in imminent danger of losing them.[45] The "soft bigotry of low expectations" that President Bush had decried in the public education system proved just as poisonous in the mortgage business.

The foreclosure rates for blacks and Hispanics were disproportionately high because blacks and Hispanics, who had comparatively poor credit ratings, were disproportionately recipients of subprime mortgages.[46] Fifty-two percent of blacks (but only 16 percent of whites) had credit scores low enough to classify them as subprime borrowers.[47] Among all borrowers in 2006, 41.5 percent of blacks and 30.9 percent of Hispanics, compared with 17.8 percent of whites, received subprime loans.[48] Across the United States, the places where subprime loans were most prevalent also had the highest foreclosure rates.[49] As Thomas Sowell wryly notes, "Being granted loans because the bank needs to meet statistical targets—quotas—in order to keep federal agencies off their backs, rather than because you are likely to be able to repay the loans, is not unequivocally a benefit to a borrower."[50]

Losing a home is a traumatic experience for anyone. But the individual tragedies of these first-time homeowners who saw their dreams go up in smoke were only part of the devastation visited on minorities by an ill-conceived progressive scheme. For those climbing the economic ladder, home ownership is the principal investment on the road to success. Prior to the 2008 crash, home ownership accounted for 63 percent of the net worth of the average African American; for whites the figure was just 38.5 percent.[51] As a result of the government-fostered housing collapse, the median net worth of black households declined by 53 percent between 2005 and 2009, while the median net worth of Hispanic households fell by 66 percent—the greatest economic blows ever delivered to these communities, according to a study by the Pew Research Center.[52] For whites, the decline was just 16 percent.[53] The Pew study further found that by 2009, the wealth gap between white households and black or Hispanic households had grown to its widest point since the government began publishing such data by ethnicity in 1984.[54]

In sum, the social justice campaign in housing, led by progressives like Clinton, Frank, and Obama, wiped out two decades of black and Hispanic efforts to rise economically. This catastrophe—which has been virtually unreported—followed what had been one of America's greatest success stories. Between 1949 and 1994, the proportion of African Americans in the middle class had nearly quadrupled, from 12 percent to 44 percent—an unprecedented advance for a previously oppressed group. The president of the National Urban League, Marc Morial, expressed the tragic irony of their fate: "These are people who played by the rules. They built wealth, went to college and had good jobs. But in a short period of time, they've fallen back."[55] "Fallen back" is putting it mildly, actually. The net worth of African Americans was cut in half, while that of Hispanics was slashed by two-thirds, because of big-government programs designed to benefit them.

Did progressive politicians learn from these mistakes, which spread misery through millions of households and set minorities back a generation? Hardly. In 2009, Representative Eddie Bernice Johnson, an African American member of the Congressional Progressive Caucus, together with fifty-one of her left-wing colleagues, proposed a new version of the CRA, which they called the Community Reinvestment Modernization Act. This progressive gem was designed "to close the wealth gap in the United States" by increasing "home ownership and small business ownership for low- and moderate-income borrowers and persons of color." The legislation sought to extend the CRA's Alice-in-Wonderland lending rules—the very rules that had led to the economic disaster—to credit unions, insurance companies, and mortgage lenders, and to apply the watered-down lending standards not only to low- and moderate-income borrowers, but to any nonwhite minorities, regardless of income.[56]

HOW PROGRESSIVES CREATED A BLACK UNDERCLASS AND CONDEMNED MILLIONS TO PERMANENT POVERTY

In the mythology of the Left, America is a class society divided into "haves" and "have-nots," but the reality is quite different. Nearly 58 percent of all taxpayers who were in the bottom income quintile in 1996 had moved into a higher income group by 2005.[57] And about half of all taxpayers in the second-lowest quintile also moved to a higher income group over the same period. Equally significant, a similar percentage of those at the top moved down. During the same period, 57 percent of those in the "top 1 percent" of all earners were in a lower income group a decade later. According to the U.S. Treasury Department, which reported these figures, they are typical and reflect the findings of previous research on income inequality over the past several decades.[58]

America is in fact a highly mobile opportunity society without meaningful hierarchies of class, race, or sex—although the gospel preached in school classrooms and from Democratic platforms across the country says just the opposite. In today's America, opportunity exists for all races and sexes, although some *individuals* might be unable or unwilling to take advantage of it. To rise economically, an individual has to acquire the necessary discipline, education, work habits, and skills. These assets are generally acquired through family upbringing and schooling, and by inhabiting a community whose culture fosters them.

The two most successful ethnic groups in America, Jews and Japanese Americans, have risen despite severe discrimination by putting great emphasis on strong family ties, education, and community support. Strong family bonds are probably paramount. As Martin Luther King observed, "Nothing is so much needed as a secure family life for a people to pull themselves out of poverty and backwardness."[59] But the majority of African Americans are now born into single-parent, female-headed households. Statistics show that a child born into such a family is *five times* more likely to be poor as an adult than a child born into a two-parent family in similar economic circumstances.[60]

This is why the soaring out-of-wedlock birthrates that began in the 1960s have had such dire repercussions for African American communities. In earlier generations, when jobs and economic opportunities were available, the working poor were able to take advantage of them and rise. But

Lyndon Johnson's War on Poverty dramatically changed family structures in poor communities, and in the African American community in particular. The new welfare programs drove fathers out of the beneficiaries' homes, creating a system of government dependency. A vast new "underclass" came into being, a class of people who were not only unemployed but unemployable.

When Johnson launched the War on Poverty in 1964, he presented it as a progressive plan to reduce dependency, "break the cycle of poverty," and make "taxpayers out of tax eaters."[61] Johnson further claimed that his programs would bring an end to the "conditions that breed despair and violence"—"ignorance, discrimination, slums, poverty, disease, not enough jobs."[62] In a famous speech in June 1965 he said, "You do not take a person who, for years, has been hobbled by chains and liberate him, bring him up to the starting line in a race and then say, 'you are free to compete with all the others,' and still justly believe that you have been completely fair."[63] Thus began an unprecedented commitment of federal funds to a wide range of measures aimed at redistributing wealth.[64]

The result? From 1965 to 2008, more than $20 trillion of taxpayer money (in constant 2008 dollars) was spent on welfare programs for the poor with little to show for it. Today the poverty rate is not appreciably better than it was fifty years ago.[65]

But it's not simply a matter of $20 trillion squandered on programs that didn't work. The reality is far worse. The War on Poverty actually reversed a trend of upward mobility for the poor. In 1965 the number of Americans living below the official poverty line was in steep decline, only about half of what it had been fifteen years earlier. This was also true of the African American poor. Between 1940 and 1960, the black poverty rate was cut nearly in half, although at the time no major anti-poverty programs had been instituted.

With the launching of the progressives' War on Poverty and the exponential growth of the welfare state, the dependency of poor Americans generally, and poor blacks in particular, rose to unprecedented levels. Between the mid-sixties and the mid-seventies, the dollar value of public housing increased fivefold, and the amount spent on food stamps tenfold. By 1974, government-provided benefits were twenty times higher than they had been in 1965.[66] Other figures were climbing as well, in particular out-of-wedlock birthrates.

Throughout the era of slavery and into the early decades of the twentieth century, most black children had grown up in two-parent households. Post–Civil War studies show that most black couples in their forties had been together for at least twenty years.[67] In Southern urban areas around 1880, the father was present in nearly three-fourths of black households; in Southern rural settings, the figure approached 86 percent.[68] As late as 1950, black women were more likely to be married than white women,[69] and in 1960 only 9 percent of black families with children were headed by a single parent.[70] By the mid-1960s, that had already begun to change.

In a famous 1965 report written at the request of President Johnson titled *The Negro Family: The Case for Action*, the social scientist and later Democratic senator Daniel Patrick Moynihan predicted that the deterioration of the Negro family, already approaching crisis proportions, would have disastrous consequences if not addressed.[71] In a subsequent article expanding on his report, Moynihan wrote: "From the wild Irish slums of the 19th-century Eastern seaboard, to the riot-torn suburbs of Los Angeles, there is one unmistakable lesson in American history: a community that allows large numbers of young men to grow up in broken families, dominated by women, never acquiring any stable relationship to male authority, never acquiring any set of rational expectations about the future—that community asks for and gets chaos. Crime, violence, unrest, disorder...are not only to be expected, they are very near to inevitable."[72]

These were prescient observations, accurately describing the social pathologies of the new underclass that government policies were about to create. Progressives responded to Moynihan's warnings by denouncing his report as "racist" and smearing him personally. The effect of their outcry was that no official government discussions of the black family could be held for the next twenty-five years.[73] Under the new welfare laws, economic incentives were offered to females to shun marriage and avoid the formation of two-parent families—exactly the opposite of what the Moynihan Report had recommended. For decades to follow, means-tested welfare programs such as food stamps, public housing, Medicaid, day care, and Temporary Assistance to Needy Families actually penalized marriage, cutting benefits by roughly 10 to 20 percent for recipients who had domestic partners.[74] Alex Roberts and David Blankenhorn offer one example of these perverse incentives: As joint incomes approach the limits for eligibility for Medicaid, "a few extra dollars in income cause thousands of dollars in benefits to be lost. What all of this means is that the two most important routes out of poverty—marriage and work—are heavily taxed...."[75]

As a result of government policies, out-of-wedlock birthrates skyrocketed. By 1976, illegitimacy rates had risen to nearly 10 percent for whites (from 3 percent in the early 1960s) and 50.3 percent for blacks (more than double the rate of 1965).[76] In 1987, for the first time in the history of any American racial or ethnic group, the birth rate for unmarried black women surpassed that for married black women.[77] Today the illegitimacy rates are 29 percent for whites and 73 percent for African Americans.[78] As the economist Walter E. Williams, an African American who rose from poverty, observes, "The welfare state has done to black Americans what slavery couldn't do, what Jim Crow couldn't do, what the harshest racism couldn't do. And that is to destroy the black family."[79]

Children raised in single-parent households are burdened with heavy social and psychological disadvantages. In 2008 the poverty rate for single parents with children was 35.6 percent, while the rate for married couples with children was 6.4 percent.[80] For Hispanics the figures were 37.5 percent and 12.8 percent; and for blacks, 35.3 percent and 6.9 percent.[81] Analyzing these figures, the Heritage Foundation's Robert Rector has testified that "the absence of marriage increases the frequency of child poverty 700 percent."[82]

Youngsters raised by single parents are more likely to be physically abused; to smoke, drink, and use drugs; to behave aggressively and violently; to engage in criminal activity; and to perform poorly in school. A study conducted by Dr. June O'Neill and Anne Hill of children with similar family structures, economic levels, and education found that the more years spent on welfare, the lower the child's IQ. A similar study by Mary Corcoran and Roger Gordon for the University of Michigan concluded that the more welfare income a family received while a boy was growing up, the lower the boy's earnings as an adult.[83]

Children in single-parent households are more than twice as likely to be arrested for a juvenile crime, twice as likely to be treated for emotional and behavioral disorders, twice as likely to be suspended or expelled from school, a third more likely to drop out of high school, three times more likely to serve jail time before age thirty, and 50 percent more likely to experience poverty as adults.[84] According to the National Fatherhood Initiative, 60 percent of rapists, 72 percent of adolescent murderers, and 70 percent of long-term prison inmates are men who grew up in fatherless homes.[85] Girls raised by single mothers are more than twice as likely themselves to bear children out of wedlock, thereby perpetuating the cycle of poverty for yet another generation.[86]

The creation of the inner-city underclass is one of the greatest crimes committed against a minority in the history of this country. Yet progressives treat the system that created the underclass as a source of pride, even as they seek to reap political gain from its disastrous results. As Thomas Sowell has observed, people who rely on government payouts "are all potential voters for those who rescued them—even if their rescuers are the reason for hard times, in the first place. Dependency pays off for politicians, even when it damages an economy or ruins a society"—or destroys the lives of the very people it was supposed to help.[87]

HOW BIG-GOVERNMENT PROGRESSIVES HAVE TAKEN AWAY THE MOST IMPORTANT RUNG OF THE ECONOMIC LADDER FOR MINORITIES AND THE POOR

The poverty rates for African Americans and Hispanics (36 percent and 35 percent, respectively) exceed those of all other racial and ethnic groups in the United States. By way of comparison, the poverty rate for whites is only 14 percent.[88] A crucial reason for this disparity is the disaster that is public school education in America's urban centers, and specifically in its inner cities.

In order to rise from poverty, the most important asset after a two-parent family is a high school diploma. America provides all its citizens with a guaranteed—indeed, required—free education from kindergarten through high school. Whether an individual manages to complete those thirteen years in the classroom has enormous implications for the rest of his life. Those who fail to finish high school will earn only a little more than half as much as those who graduate.[89] People who receive a high school diploma and also wait until they are twenty years old and married before having their first child are *ten times* less likely to be poor than those who do not graduate and who have children out of wedlock—regardless of race or ethnicity.[90]

Almost half of black and Hispanic students in public schools fail to earn a diploma.[91] The dropout rates are especially high in urban areas with large minority populations, including such academic disaster zones as Washington, D.C. (57 percent), Trenton (59 percent), Camden (61.4 percent), Baltimore (65.4 percent), Cleveland (65.9 percent), and Detroit (75.1 percent).[92] These dropouts miss out on the American dream and are condemned to spend their lives in poverty.

A substantial percentage of black and Hispanic students who do manage to graduate are unable to read their own diplomas. Overall, black high school graduates are four academic years behind their white counterparts in achievement levels.[93] In the class of 2011, for example, only 11 percent of blacks and 15 percent of Hispanics were proficient in math, as compared with 42 percent of whites. Similarly, just 13 percent of blacks and 4 percent of Hispanics were proficient in reading, versus 40 percent of whites.[94] Lydia G. Segal, a political science professor, summed up the sad state of affairs in her book *Battling Corruption in America's Public Schools*: "It is in cities such as New York, Chicago, Los Angeles, Detroit, and Philadelphia where the largest numbers of children cannot read, write, and compute at acceptable levels and where racial gaps between whites and blacks and Latinos are widest. It is in large cities that minority boys in particular, trapped in poor schools, have the greatest chance of flunking out and getting sucked into the downward spiral of crime and prison."[95]

The public schools in America's largest inner cities—schools that year in and year out fail to educate poor minority children—have been the exclusive domain of big-government Democrats for decades.[96] Progressives have fought tooth and nail to prevent bad teachers from being fired and good teachers from being rewarded. They have spent millions on electoral campaigns to deny inner-city parents access to voucher programs that would provide scholarships for their children to attend schools that would educate them. These same progressives, fully aware of the bankruptcy of public education, send their own children to expensive private schools, where they will get the education unavailable in public schools. When Vice President Al Gore, a supporter of teachers' unions and an opponent of school vouchers, was asked why he opposed school vouchers for black children while sending his own son to St. Alban's, the most exclusive private school in Washington, he admitted, "If I was the parent of a child who went to an inner-city school that was failing ... I might be for vouchers, too."[97]

To defend an educational system that has extinguished the hopes of millions of poor black and Hispanic children, progressives insist that the problem of public education is not enough money. The claim is brazenly false. American taxpayers spend $600 billion per year on public elementary and secondary schools,[98] and the national average per-pupil expenditure is at an all-time high of $10,905[99]—a nearly fourfold increase (in constant present-day dollars) since 1961.[100] Detroit spends about $15,945 per public school pupil.[101] Yet according to the U.S. Education Department's National Assessment of Educational Progress, fourth and eighth graders in that city's public schools in 2010 were reading at a level that was 73 percent below the national average.[102] Their math scores in 2011 were the lowest ever recorded in the forty-year history of the test.[103] In Trenton, New Jersey, whose population is more than 80 percent black and Hispanic,[104] the government spends $20,663 per pupil, while the citywide high school graduation rate is a mere 41 percent.[105] In Camden, New Jersey, where nearly 90 percent of the residents are black or Hispanic,[106] the situation is even worse. Camden spends $15,961 per pupil, yet only 38.6 percent of its public school children ever obtain a high school diploma.[107]

A good education—let alone what passes for an education in these failed public schools—should not be so expensive. If there are thirty students to a classroom, per-pupil spending of $16,000 to $20,000 per child—as in Detroit, Trenton, and Camden—comes to more than half a million dollars per class. With that kind of money, how difficult should it be to teach thirty students to read and write and do basic math over the course of thirteen years? But public schools place students so far down on their list of priorities and so much of the education dollar is spent on bloated bureaucracies and six-figure-income administrators that even this modest task is beyond them, no matter how much money they are able to tax out of working Americans.

Wasting money on administrators of failing schools is a trend that has been gaining momentum. In California, for instance, superintendents and other administrators earned an average of $168,000 in base pay in 2010—an increase of 56 percent from a decade earlier.[108] In Florida, 946 school administrators earned at least $100,000 each in 2010—an 818 percent increase in the number of six-figure salaries since 2005. Florida's classroom teachers did not participate in this windfall, as they were paid an average of $47,000 each (the equivalent of about $60,000 if they worked a full calendar year).[109] The gravy train for public school administrators does not end when their workdays are over. In California, between 2005 and 2011, the number of education professionals receiving $100,000-plus annual pensions rose by 650 percent, from 700 to 5,400.[110]

Even when it recognizes its own failures, government cannot reverse them. The federal government has poured hundreds of billions of extra dollars into "Title I" schools—schools it actually designates as "failed"—with nothing to show for its investment.[111] The problem is not money. The problem is that these schools are a monopoly run for the benefit of the teachers and their unions with no penalties for failure and no incentives to change. Every year, government schools blight the lives of millions upon millions of poor black and Hispanic children. This scandal is the responsibility of big-government progressives, and it has been ongoing for half a century with no remedy in sight.

AFFIRMATIVE ACTION RACE PREFERENCES DAMAGE THE LIVES OF AFRICAN AMERICANS

Martin Luther King did not demand lower standards so that African Americans could achieve "equality." His "dream" was a single standard for all Americans. To his fellow blacks he said, "The Negro must work a little harder than the white man, for he who gets behind must run a little harder or forever remain behind."[112] Shelby Steele, an African American writer on civil rights, put it this way: "No one ever learned to jump higher by lowering the bar."[113] Yet that is exactly what "affirmative action" policies propose.

The term entered the national vocabulary on March 6, 1961, when President Kennedy issued Executive Order 10925, stating that federally funded projects should "take affirmative action" to ensure that their hiring and employment practices were untainted by bias regarding "race, color, creed, or national origin."[114] The affirmative action that Kennedy proposed was synonymous with equal opportunity, not the rigged system of racial preferences it has become. It was not long, however, before organizations on the Left were demanding new definitions of affirmative action. The National Urban League, the Congress of Racial Equality, and the NAACP all pressed for reforms requiring employers to adopt race preferences and quotas in their hiring and promotions as a way of compensating blacks for past discrimination.[115] Encouraging these demands, President Johnson declared in 1965 that it was "not enough just to open the gates of opportunity"; the ultimate goal of government regulations should be to achieve "equality as a fact and as a result."[116]

At the same time, the Equal Employment Opportunity Commission changed the legal standards by which employment discrimination was judged. No longer was proof of bias in hiring and promotion the standard. Now disparities in outcomes became prima facie evidence of such discrimination, whether or not individual achievements and efforts may have affected them.[117] By the 1970s, this had become the national norm, as the government's newly created civil rights divisions compelled both private and public institutions to give preference to blacks in order to increase their representation in the workplace and in academic institutions. Thus a racially discriminatory standard was reintroduced into America's laws and institutions. Much has been written about the injustices and resentments to which these new practices gave rise. But little attention has been paid to the destructive consequences of the new federally sanctioned discrimination to African Americans themselves.

These consequences were crystallized in the landmark Supreme Court decision in *Regents of the University of California v. Bakke* (1977). The UC Davis medical school reserved sixteen places in each class for "qualified" black and Hispanic students. Allan Bakke, who was white, was twice rejected for admission, despite grades and Medical College Admissions Test scores that exceeded those of any of the black and Hispanic students against whom he was competing for admission.[118]

Bakke sued the university for discrimination and won his case in state court, where a judge ruled that race could not be used as a factor in admissions decisions. The case ended up before the U.S. Supreme Court, which ruled, in June 1978, that schools *could* consider race as one factor (termed a "plus" factor) in the admissions process, but also found that Bakke had been discriminated against.[119] One of the black students admitted to UC Davis instead of Allan Bakke was Patrick Chavis.[120] In years to come, he was hailed by progressive luminaries like Senator Ted Kennedy as a "perfect example" of how affirmative action worked, because he had gone on to become a "poor-folks' doctor" in a minority neighborhood.[121] Kennedy's encomium, however, was a triumph of political fiction over disturbing real-world facts.[122] Chavis did set up his practice in South-Central Los Angeles, where his services were indeed available to low-income blacks. His motives, however, were far from humanitarian, and his services even less so. To increase his income, he included cosmetic surgery in his practice, a treatment for which he was not properly trained, with disastrous, and in one case fatal, consequences for his patients. In 1997 Chavis was stripped of his medical license after a medical board found him negligent and incompetent. In numerous cases brought before the board, Chavis was found guilty of demonstrating "poor impulse control and insensitivity to patients' pain."[123]

Chavis's story was systematically buried and explained away by supporters of affirmative action, who attributed his malpractice to personal problems rather than the system that had credentialed him. But no attempt has been made to assess the damage that credentialing unqualified physicians may have done to patients, while it is indisputable that the test scores of blacks who are accepted to medical schools are substantially lower on average than those of whites who are rejected. At the University of Maryland School of Medicine in 2000, for example, blacks with college GPAs of B or B+ and MCAT scores in the bottom half of all test takers had a 70 percent likelihood of admission, while for whites and Asians the figure was 2 percent.[124] Not surprisingly, among blacks who do succeed in getting admitted to medical school, the failure rate is high. Whereas approximately 85 percent of white medical school students graduate within four years, the figure for blacks is less than 60 percent.[125] The African Americans who manage to become doctors are less likely than their white counterparts to become board certified in every specialty choice categories other than family medicine.[126]

Double standards are also ubiquitous in law schools. In the early 1990s, blacks were admitted to top law schools at a rate 17.5 times what it would have been under race-neutral rules.[127] At the University of Virginia Law School in 1998, black in-state male applicants with a Law School Admissions Test score of 160 and a GPA of 3.25 had a 96 percent chance of admission, in contrast to the 3 percent chance of similarly qualified Hispanic and white applicants. The odds that a given black applicant would be admitted in preference to an equally qualified white applicant at Virginia were almost 650 to 1 in favor of the black applicant.[128] In 2006 a white resident who applied for admission to the University of Arizona Law School with the same credentials as the average black resident had a 5 percent chance of admission. Those credentials gave the black student a 93 percent chance of admission.[129]

No one knows how many patients or legal clients, both black and white, have suffered from professional incompetence because of the dismantling of standards that had been developed over generations for the public's protection. The chief victims of affirmative action, however, are the African Americans who ought to have benefited from racial preferences.[130] Elite schools not only rig their admissions standards but recruit unqualified minority students to fill their racial quotas. However satisfying the results might be for school administrators, they are devastating for black students who could have succeeded at non-elite schools but were enticed into collegiate experiences where they failed instead.[131]

Throughout the 1980s, affirmative action became codified in university admissions policies across the United States. Though black students' median SAT scores in any given year were (and still are) generally two hundred points lower than the median scores of their white peers, the former were admitted to virtually all academically competitive schools at much higher rates. In their important study of the long-term effects of affirmative action, *The Shape of the River*, William Bowen, a former president of Princeton, and Derek Bok, a former president of Harvard, reported that at five of America's top universities, black applicants whose SAT scores fell within the 1200 to 1249 range had a 60 percent chance of admission, whereas whites with similar scores had just a 19 percent chance.[132]

The consequence of these ill-thought-out discriminatory schemes was an abnormally high failure and dropout rate for the black students who were selected to benefit from the programs. A 2008 study by the think tank Education Sector reported that black students were 2.5 times more likely to enroll at a college where they had a 70 percent chance of dropping out than at a college where they had a 70 percent chance of graduating.[133] Not surprisingly, racial disparities in graduation rates correspond closely to the degree of racial preference in a given school's admissions policies. For example, one study found that black students at the University of Colorado at Boulder, whose SAT scores were typically at least 200 points lower than those of their white peers, had a graduation rate of just 39 percent, compared with 72 percent for white students. By contrast, at the University of Colorado at Denver (a second-tier school), where the black-white SAT disparity was a negligible thirty points, the graduation rates for blacks and whites were almost identical.[134]

In evaluating the effects of preferential admissions policies, it is necessary to consider the lost opportunities for those minority students who were directed to the wrong schools in order to satisfy the progressive agenda. Thomas Sowell, who has published studies on worldwide affirmative action policies, observes that these are "casualties of the double-standards admissions process," representing "the 'collateral damage' of affirmative action." Such students "would have been far better off succeeding on some campus where the admissions standards matched their academic background and capabilities."[135]

As in undergraduate education, preferential admissions to law schools have many negative consequences for African American students. From the outset of their legal studies, they receive much lower grades than their white peers. More than half of black first-year law students rank in the bottom tenth of their classes academically, while only 8 percent reach even the top half of their classes.[136] Black students drop out of law school at nearly twice the rate of their white peers.[137] African Americans who manage to complete their legal education are two to four times more likely than whites to fail the bar examination on their first try, and two to seven times more likely never to pass the bar at all.[138] In short, while law school administrators can boast that they have made their student bodies "diverse," they have also burdened African American students with unnecessary life-changing failures by mismatching them with schools they could not succeed in and circumventing standards that were designed to prevent that result.

Apart from the injustices done to black and nonblack students alike, there is the question of whether such policies were necessary in the first place—even as temporary measures to rectify past discrimination. Self-serving promoters of racial preferences—and black failure—justify their actions by ignoring the remarkable progress that African Americans had made in the era before affirmative action, when they relied on the principle of working harder against greater odds, as Martin Luther King advised. Between 1940 and 1960, when there were no affirmative action programs, African Americans improved their social and economic position faster than they did after the passage of the 1964 Civil Rights Act or after racial preferences were introduced in the 1970s in the guise of affirmative action.

In 1940 only 10 percent of African American males held middle-class jobs, but that figure had more than doubled to 23 percent by 1960. Between 1940 and 1950, the earnings of the average African American male, in real dollars adjusted for inflation, grew by a remarkable 75 percent (about twice the rate at which white male incomes grew) and increased by another 45 percent during the 1950s. By 1960, male incomes among African Americans were 2.5 times greater than they had been twenty years earlier, and female incomes were 2.3 times greater.[139] As we have seen, in the two decades prior to the creation of the welfare system, the poverty rate among African Americans had virtually been cut in half. In the era of the progressive "War on Poverty," however, there was little if any improvement at all in the statistical rates, while a new class of poor people with many new burdens was created by these government programs.

Blacks' prosperity was growing in other ways before the advent of affirmative action and the welfare state. For instance, between 1940 and 1960 the proportion of African Americans who owned homes rose by 65 percent, compared with a 41 percent rise for whites. In 1940 African American life expectancy at birth was just fifty-three years, eleven years less than whites. By 1960 African American life expectancy had risen by ten and a half years, while white life expectancy had increased by only half as much. During that same twenty-year period, the percentage of African Americans who attained high school diplomas more than tripled, while the corresponding figure for whites grew at only one-fifth that rate.[140] In short, the failures inflicted on African Americans by government programs to promote "diversity" and equality could have been avoided, while the principal beneficiaries were white administrators, government officials, and progressive activists who could feel good about themselves.

CONCLUSION

The government campaigns that changed the rules so that the poor— and especially the minority poor—could buy homes they couldn't afford led to the greatest collapse of home values since the Great Depression. It caused untold trauma to poor families who lost their homes through foreclosure and wiped out half the net worth of middle class African Americans, who had worked hard to rise out of the poverty of their parents' generation. Massive government welfare programs destroyed inner-city black families and created a black underclass permanently dependent on government handouts, beset by out-of-control crime rates and rampant substance abuse, and deprived of any real prospect of rising out of poverty as previous generations had done. Government monopolies in public education, run as lifetime jobs programs for adults with no rewards for success or punishments for failure, destroyed a school system that had once been the ladder to success for America's immigrant poor. Racial preference programs disguised as affirmative action reintroduced racial categories into America's public life, produced unnecessary failure rates among minority students, and spread incompetence through civic institutions. Progressive remedies have condemned millions of poor black and Hispanic children to lives of poverty and hopelessness and damaged the lives of countless others.

The progressive axiom that it takes a government to raise a child has been shown in practice to be a perverse untruth. Government can destroy a child. It can destroy entire communities. Given enough latitude and time, and enough power to work with, it can destroy a nation.

CHAPTER SEVEN

THE TEA PARTY AND THE GOP: CAN THIS MARRIAGE SURVIVE?

My answer is: it better. The White House is occupied by a lifelong anti-American radical who has done more to bankrupt this nation's economy, take us down as a military power, and destroy individual liberty than anyone would have thought possible when he took office in January 2009. And it's worse than that. Obama is the head of a Democratic Party that has moved so far to the left over the last forty-six years that it has become anti–free market, anti-individualist, anti-constitutionalist, and unready to defend America's sovereign interests at home and abroad. We cannot afford to let such a party run our government for another four or eight years. The world cannot afford it.

So how do we hold together the conservative coalition opposing this national suicide? How do we make this marriage survive? First of all, by recognizing that the basic difference between the Tea Party and the Republican Party is a matter of tactics and temperament, not policy and ideology. To understand what I mean by this, go back to the flashpoint that made the possibility of a Republican schism a topic of discussion: the government shutdown supposedly perpetrated by the Tea Party hero Senator Ted Cruz of Texas. I probably should acknowledge here that I am a huge fan of what the Tea Party represents, though not always what it does. I believe the emergence of the Tea Party is the most important political development in conservatism in the last twenty-five years and is possibly the last, best hope for our country. And I believe that Ted Cruz is a worthy conservative leader.

The government shutdown was allegedly the result of Senator Cruz's decision to filibuster a continuing resolution to fund the government. In fact, the House had already passed a resolution to fund the government—just not Obamacare. In the Senate, Democratic majority leader Harry Reid stripped the Obamacare-funding ban from the House bill. Cruz's one-man filibuster was designed to express his opposition both to Reid and to the Republicans who voted to fund Obamacare rather than join him. What ensued was Republicans attacking each other instead of the real culprits.

You might ask yourself this question: What would have happened if the Republican Party and the Tea Party and the big political action committees run by Karl Rove and the Koch brothers had funded a $30 million campaign to put the blame on Obama and Reid, where it belonged? There was no such campaign. Instead of everyone on our side's taking the fight to the enemy camp, we got the kind of circular firing squad that we on the Right are so good at and that continually sets us back.

Here's a second important point that applies to all the frictions between Tea Partiers and Republican regulars. The conflict within the Right about the Obama shutdown was not about policy. It was about tactics. Every Republican in Congress, without exception, is opposed to Obamacare. Not a single Republican legislator voted for it. Not a single Republican legislator would support it. The issue is how best to defeat the Democrats and repeal a monstrous law. Understanding that conservatives disagree on tactics, not fundamentals, is crucial to keeping the marriage alive. A tactical difference is no grounds for divorce.

There is a difference between politics, which is about electoral conflict, and policy, which is about governing. Republicans and conservatives are good at policy; they are not so good at politics. That's unfortunate, because politics is the only way you get to make policy. Do we repeal Obamacare by obstructing it at every turn? Or do we repeal it by lying low until we have a majority and abolishing it at a stroke? And if we lie low, will that demoralize our troops, who will see us as compromisers and appeasers, ruining our chance of ever winning a majority and accomplishing our goal? These are the questions that divide us. They are legitimate questions and—excuse me for being blunt about this—no one knows the answers. Politics is always a gamble. No one can be sure what tactic will succeed, which is why we have to respect each other and keep our coalition strong, even when we disagree.

I said we are not good at politics. Actually we're pretty terrible at politics. Whenever a Republican and a Democrat square off, it's Godzilla versus Bambi. They call us racists, sexists, homophobes, and selfish pigs, and we call them...liberals. Who's going to win that argument? They spend their political dollars calling us names and shredding our reputations; we spend ours explaining why the complicated solutions we propose will work and why theirs won't. But when you are being called a racist, an enemy of women, and a greedy SOB, who will listen to your ideas about the budget? Who is going to believe you when all your motives are portrayed as vile?

This is the problem that not only Republicans but also Tea Partiers and conservatives in general have failed to address. It is why the Democratic Party, which supports policies that are morally repugnant and have also failed on an epic scale, still wins elections. Medicare is bankrupt and a mess; Social Security is bankrupt and a mess; the War on Poverty is a twenty-trillion-dollar catastrophe that has created worse poverty than it was designed to cure—and yet Democrats can still propose and pass the biggest socialist entitlement and redistributionist scheme ever and get away with it. Until Republicans and Tea Partiers are willing to fight fire with fire, these circumstances are not going to change. Twenty-five years after the most oppressive empire in human history collapsed because socialist economics don't work, 49 percent of American youth, according to a recent Pew poll, think socialism is a good system.[1] That's a political failure on our part. We won the Cold War, but we didn't drive the stake through the Communist heart. As a result, the vampire of "social justice" has risen to fight another day.

Another way of stating the problem is that the Republican Party—like conservatives generally—is guided by a business mentality, whereas the Left's mentality is missionary. Let me explain what I mean by this. Democrats, progressives, and so-called liberals see themselves as social redeemers. They don't approach social problems pragmatically, looking for ways to improve this situation or that, except as a political expedient—a means to a greater end. When they approach social problems, it is with an eye to *changing the world*. As First Lady Hillary Clinton said, in 1993, "Let us be willing to remold society by redefining what it means to be a human being in the twentieth century, moving into a new millennium."[2]

Remold society by redefining what it means to be human. No Republican in his right mind thinks like that. On the eve of his election, Barack Obama said, "We are five days away from fundamentally transforming the United States of America." People who understand the American political system— and respect it—don't think like that. This is the thought pattern of radical progressives who believe that they are "on the right side of history," that the moral arc of the universe itself "is bent towards justice"—a justice that coincides with their own views.[3]

The Democratic Party has become an anti-democratic party and therefore a dangerous one. It is driven by the missionary Left, backed by the billions of George Soros and his friends in what I call the "Shadow Party,"[4] and it regards politics as war conducted by other means. That is why Democrats can say—and believe—that Republicans are conducting wars against women, minorities, and the poor, while Republicans refer to them as liberals and patiently explain to them why their policies won't work. If explaining why their policies won't work were politically effective, they'd be out of business already. Socialism doesn't work; central planning doesn't work. These very ideas ruined whole continents.

Why haven't Democrats learned from that? Because they are missionaries, and their politics is a religion that provides them with a meaning for their existence. Progressives are the prophets of a social redemption, a future in which the meaning of being human has been redefined and social justice prevails. They cannot give up the hope that inspires them, that provides their own lives with meaning, and they dismiss (or find a way around) the unpalatable facts. The cause is too noble to fail, so every failure along the way is merely a setback or a glitch, never a reason to abandon the cause. After a century of corpses and ruined continents, people not blinded by faith understand that the dreams of socialism are delusional and dangerous. Yet these are the fantasies that drive the Democratic Party today.

In contrast to this missionary ardor, the business mentality of conservatives is pragmatic, and their expectations are modest. Conservatives are not striving for a future ideal but are trying to make the best out of life for the human beings who inhabit the world now and to leave it in reasonably good condition for those who come after. Conservatism is mindful of the limits of human capabilities. When a businessman is delusional, when his expectations exceed the capacities of the marketplace, he is punished by the market and punished without mercy. No such obstacles lie in the path of the pursuers of bad ideas.

To succeed, a business must meet the expectations of others. Therefore, where possible, it wants to avoid conflict and the alienation of others; it is looking to maximize customers and expand markets, and thus to make deals. A businessman would rather buy you out or merge with you than crush you. Whenever obstacles present themselves, it is cheaper, and in the long run more productive, to compromise and find a way around them.

This is the mentality of the Republican Party's Washington insiders. You can understand the schism between the Tea Party and the Republican Party if you keep in mind that the Tea Party, though composed of conservatives, is driven more by a missionary mentality, while the Republican Party is more like a business establishment with a businessman's temperament and approach. Speaker of the House John Boehner and Senate minority leader Mitch McConnell are dealmakers, not game changers.

The problem for conservatives is that the business mentality is a handicap when the opposition is a missionary party. If your opponents view politics as war and are out for your blood, an equal and opposing force—a missionary force—may be required to defeat them. The grassroots understands this. That's why the Tea Party was born and why a maverick like Ted Cruz was able to defeat the establishment's anointed candidate in the most important Republican state and become its senator.

While the Tea Party is a missionary party, its mission is different from that of the political Left. It does not seek to create a new race of human beings or a new social order. Its mission is closer to the realism of business. It seeks to defend something familiar and real—a Constitution that has been shredded, a culture that has been betrayed, and an economy that is heading for bankruptcy. This doesn't mean that Tea Partiers should be unmindful of the dangers that missionary ideas bring with them. Good principles don't guarantee good candidates or winning politics. Some Tea Party losses in 2012, which hurt the conservative cause and deprived Republicans of a Senate majority, could have been avoided if the distinctions were kept in mind.

The very fact that the Tea Party is missionary, that it is organized as a cause, makes its demands and actions seem impractical and even extreme to business-as-usual Republicans. This is inevitable. In order to change things, you have to take positions that seem unrealistic and maybe even extreme. That is the nature of change, and the Tea Party is about change. And in fact it is already changing something—the Republican Party. Without the Tea Party, there would be no Senator Cruz, no Senator Paul, no Senator Lee. If the Tea Party were not challenging the Republican establishment, it would have no reason for being.

In my view Ted Cruz's stand on the Senate floor did not injure the chances of a Republican victory in 2014; it enhanced them. It did so because it lit a fire in the Republican base and showed the rank and file that there were Republicans who were ready to fight, who weren't cowed by Democratic threats. This is what conservative voters most want to see. Both

McCain and Romney lost because they failed to inspire the passion among Republican voters that gets them to the polls. Too many Republicans—too many conservatives—sat the election out. And why not, since both McCain and Romney assured them that Obama was "a good man." No, he isn't. He's a compulsive, brazen liar and a human wrecking ball, bent on destroying the foundations of a great nation.

An important question for conservatives is whether the Tea Party can succeed as a caucus within the Republican Party and, if so, what changes it can achieve. Can Republicans like Boehner and McConnell—if they're not unseated in primaries or by votes in their caucuses—be changed? Tea Partiers may think that's a silly question. Of course they won't change. Such men have the business mentality I've been talking about—that's the problem. But wait. Precisely because they have that business mentality, they appreciate the realities of power. If the grassroots mobilizes and the Tea Party achieves critical mass, Boehner and McConnell *can* be changed. That's what politics is about.

In fact, that is precisely the way the Democratic Party was changed over the last five decades. Grassroots extremists of the Left first attacked the party and then infiltrated it. The radicals began their infiltration during the McGovern presidential campaign of 1972. Within just a few years, they were able to transform it from the party of John F. Kennedy into the party of Barack Obama.

So how do conservatives and Republicans fight fire with fire? How do we change from a debating society that keeps wondering why the Democrats won't engage us like gentlemen to a political force that can defeat their politics of personal and political destruction? To put it another way, how do we develop a political weapon that matches and neutralizes theirs, in particular the claim that we are waging a war against women, minorities, and the poor?

It is not that difficult if you are prepared to be aggressive, if you are willing to match their rhetoric and style—to punch them in the mouth and make them forget their game plan, as a Democratic strategist once advised.

I have made the point before, but in my experience you have to repeat the obvious. Shove their victims in their faces. The plight of Detroit, which is 85 percent black, is emblematic of what happens when Democrats get their way. In fifty years, Democrats have reduced Detroit from the richest city in the country to a byword for urban blight and human despair. With their plans for social justice, they turned the city into a cesspool of racial politics and antibusiness practices. In one generation they bankrupted America's industrial jewel and ruined it. That's the truth of it. A third of Detroit's population is on welfare; half is unemployed. It is now the poorest large city in America. Over a million people—more than half its one-time population—have left. Everyone who can has fled. Detroit is now a giant slum of human misery and hopelessness. Democrats did it. Democrats are Detroit's slumlords. Their racist policies have reduced a once-great city to abject squalor. It is a cynical lie for Democrats to claim that they are interested in the well-being of minorities and the poor. Republicans must not let them get away with it.

Fighting fire with fire means throwing the Democrats' atrocities against black and brown Americans in their faces every time they open their mouths. It means condemning them for destroying the lives of millions of poor black and Hispanic children. It means taking up the cause of the victims and indicting the progressive perpetrators. The one thing it does *not* mean is business as usual.

PART TWO

CHAPTER EIGHT

THE ART OF POLITICAL WAR

*This was originally published in 1999, in pamphlet form, by
American Strategies, Inc.*

The Republican Party claims to be the party of personal responsibility, yet it has become a party that takes no responsibility for the predicaments it finds itself in. Instead, Republicans blame bias in the media, or the liar in the White House, or their unprincipled opponents, or even the immorality of the American people to explain their defeats.

How can you win in American politics if you have contempt for the judgment of the American people? You can't.

The greatest political deficiency of the Republican Party today is lack of respect for the common sense of the American people. "Respect" in this context does not mean following polls or focus groups or putting one's finger slavishly to the winds. It means that what is right politically (within a constitutional framework and consistent with deeply held principles) produces electoral majorities.

Liberals also fail to understand this. But they were fortunate to have in Bill Clinton a leader who did, who disregarded their advice, and who used his power as the head of their party to force them to pay heed to the voice of the people. The reason Bill Clinton survived his impeachment, riding high in the polls, is that he understood what the electorate wanted and gave it to them (or least made them think he had).

Despite a flawed presidency and the worst White House scandal since Watergate, Clinton was able to sustain his popularity by remaking the Democrat Party both tactically and ideologically, much against its will. While the liberal majority in his party dug in their heels and opposed free trade, welfare reform, balanced budgets, and a tough stance on crime, Clinton pursued a "triangulation" strategy with Republicans to do just the opposite.

As a result, in the public's mind the Clinton Democrats appear to be the party of economic vibrancy, anticrime laws, welfare reform laws, budget surpluses, and free trade. That's what the American people want, and that's what they believe Clinton has delivered. Unless Republicans change their strategy and tactics to adapt to this reality, they are destined for political irrelevance. They cannot fight past wars and expect to win present battles.

Republicans will ask how can we in good conscience respect the judgment of the American people when they failed to support the impeachment and removal of a corrupt president? The question, of course, is rhetorical. The only possible answer is: Blame the people. But if conservatives really believe in America's constitutional order, their first political article of faith surely must be this: The people are sovereign.

Where complex issues of government, society, and law are concerned, truth is elusive. Conservatives ought to know that no one has a monopoly on truth, least of all politicians in government. Should the president be impeached? Is the minimum wage a boon to workers, or does it eliminate jobs? We think we know what is true, but we also know we may be wrong. This humility is what makes conservatives, or should make them, small "d" democrats. We do not believe in rule by the anointed; we do not believe in the divine right of the infallible.

Democracy arbitrates life's uncertainties through electoral pluralities. In America, nobody gets to decide what's true and what's false, what's right and what's wrong, without the consent—or at least the tolerance—of a plurality of the American electorate. If the electorate is wrong, only the electorate can remedy its error. In a democracy, appropriate respect for the people's judgment is a moral imperative, not just a political necessity. If you don't have faith in the long-term good sense of the American public, then you don't really have faith in the system the Founders established.

IT'S THE POLITICS, STUPID

During the impeachment debate, the American people knew that Bill Clinton was corrupt and despised him as a person even as they did not want him removed from office. Most Americans knew he was guilty of perjury, but they were reluctant to see him impeached.

Clinton escaped judgment because he based his defense on conservative principles and because Republicans were silent for eight months and allowed him to define the issues. When Republicans finally found their collective voice, they talked past the immediate concerns of the American electorate and based their prosecution on issues that were too complex for the public to digest.

It's the politics, stupid.

For eight months between the time Monica Lewinsky surfaced and President Clinton admitted their relationship, Republicans said nothing about the developing sex scandal. Meanwhile, the White House launched its own national campaign to define the issues for the American public. Republican silence was based on the hope that Clinton Democrats would self-destruct and the fear that Republicans couldn't handle the issue without shooting themselves in the foot. The two sentiments had the same reasoning behind them: Republicans were afraid to fight the political battle. It was because Republicans did not trust themselves to frame the scandal to their advantage that they hoped for a Democratic implosion.

In political warfare, if only one side is shooting, the other side will soon be dead. While Republicans vacated the battlefield from January to August 1999, the president's allies portrayed him as a victim of government abuse. They defined the issues surrounding the investigation as government invasion of privacy (a conservative principle) and government prosecutors out of control (a conservative concern). That Americans responded to this appeal should have been cause for conservative satisfaction, not dismay. It is not the American people that Republicans should blame for their failure to remove the president. They should blame their own political ineptitude.

When Republicans finally did make their case, they built their arguments on legalistic grounds that were either unintelligible to the majority of the electorate, or were based on liberal principles they had themselves opposed—and which the public rejected.

Although impeachment is a political process conducted by the legislative branch, Republicans notably failed to focus on a *political* case for the removal of the president. Instead, Republicans relied on interpretations of the law and on legal arguments arising from the failed Paula Jones suit to make their case for removal.

A statute allowing the court to investigate the personal sexual histories of defendants in sexual harassment cases led to the discovery of Monica Lewinsky. This was a radical law, departing from the norms of American justice, which previously enshrined the principle that a defendant is presumed innocent until proved guilty. Even accused killers have the right to be tried for the charges at hand rather than for what they may have been convicted of doing in the past. But radical sexual harassment law allows courts to dredge up not only past *convictions* (of which Clinton had none), but past *alleged* crimes as well. Once allegations are introduced into the record, and a "pattern" is established, the presumption of guilt can become overwhelming—which is why American law, before it was corrupted by feminist theories, ruled out such practices.

"Sexual McCarthyism"—a charge that Democrats successfully used against the Republican prosecutors—was in fact an invention of the radical Left. As a consequence of Republicans' folly in embracing their enemies' philosophy, the entire impeachment debate was framed by sexual harassment laws that were designed by radical feminists and that conservatives had always opposed.

Furthermore, the impeachment debate revolved around matters only constitutional experts and trial lawyers could properly discuss with any claim to authority: Was the president's testimony in a sexual harassment case material or not? Was testimony in that same case about matters that should be private? What constitutes perjury? What is obstruction? What are impeachable offenses? Because the debate was legalistic, many people thought it was over their heads or just plain irrelevant, particularly since Republicans were constantly reminding them that impeachment was a political process and political jurors would render the verdict.

In other words, Republicans chose to fight on grounds where the public could not (or would not) follow them. Because the *legalistic* arguments of the Republicans failed to gain traction with a majority of the public, the Democrats' *political* arguments prevailed. The president's privacy had been invaded; government prosecutors had abused their power; a sex act was not a reason to remove a president the people had elected. A skeptical public was readily persuaded that the president was a victim of partisan attacks. In political terms, "victims" are underdogs, little guys—that is, the people themselves. In a democratic political contest, the winner is the one who persuades the people to identify with him. In a democracy, this is the first—and perhaps only—principle of political war: the side of the underdog, which is the side of the people, wins.

In the impeachment conflict, sound Democrat political strategy was reinforced by a full-employment economy, a soaring Dow, positive social trends (declining crime rates, increasing morality indexes), and no clear political framing of the case for removal. In these circumstances, the public's (conservative) response of sticking with a twice-elected sitting president was perfectly understandable, even reassuring.

Of course, the Democratic campaign in defense of the president was a remarkable display of hypocrisy and double-talk, which is to say it was a virtuoso demonstration of how a purely political strategy was able to serve a political party in grave difficulty. Thanks to a superior grasp of political strategy, the actual inventors of sexual McCarthyism were able to pin the label on Republicans. Liberals who had spent four decades rewriting the Constitution suddenly emerged as the champions of original intent ("the Constitutional bar for high crimes has not been met"). The veterans of half a century of antiwar crusades against the American military became overnight enthusiasts of wag-the-dog missile strikes in the Sudan, Afghanistan, and Iraq.[1] The creators of the special prosecutor's office, who had ruthlessly used its powers to persecute three Republican presidents, became instant critics of prosecutorial excess and the loudest proponents of reform.

As the party of bankrupt principles, discredited policies, and two-faced political arguments, the Democrats have dramatically demonstrated how effective the art of political war can be in the hands of a party that understands its principles. In contrast, an illustration of Republicans' idea of political warfare is the following slogan posted on a closed-circuit television program that the Republican Policy Committee produces for House members: "Republicans target the problems; Democrats target the politics."

There could hardly be a more succinct explanation of why Republicans are so regularly routed by their Democrat adversaries in battles like the impeachment process. It's the politics, stupid. If you don't focus on winning the political battle, you don't get to target the problems.

Before Republicans can begin to change this situation, they need to stop whining that life is unfair, that Bill Clinton "stole" their programs, and that Democrats don't play by the rules. They need to stop complaining that Democrats are unprincipled or that they follow a party line. (Of course they do. It's the politics, stupid.) They need to accept that Democrats are going to practice the politics of personal destruction and attribute to Republicans the sins they themselves have committed. They do it because that's the way they win.

When Republicans complain about forces they can't control, they behave like victims and give up the power to determine their fate. Democrats will be Democrats. They will be unprincipled and lie. Republicans can hope Democrats will behave better than this, but if Republicans go into battle expecting Democrats to be better than they are, they will only be setting themselves up for political ambush. Instead of complaining about others, Republicans should be asking themselves: How do they do it? How do they get away with it? What do they know that makes them able to package a bankrupt political agenda and sell it successfully to the American voter?

THE PRINCIPLES

Here are the principles of political war that the Left understands, but conservatives do not:

1. Politics is war conducted by other means.
2. Politics is a war of position.
3. In political warfare, the aggressor usually prevails.
4. Position is defined by fear and hope.
5. The weapons of politics are symbols that evoke fear and hope.
6. Victory lies on the side of the people.

First, a caveat. Politics is contextual: rules cannot be applied rigidly and succeed. If it is true that the aggressor usually prevails, there are times when he will not, and it is absolutely crucial to recognize them. If politics is war, it is also true that a war mentality produces sanctimony and self-serious moralizing, which can be deadly. To be effective, you need to get serious and lighten up at the same time. If politics is war, it's also a combination of blackjack, craps, and poker. Politically, it is better to be seen as a peacemaker than as a warmonger. But it is not always possible. If forced to fight, then fight to win.

1. POLITICS IS WAR CONDUCTED BY OTHER MEANS

In political warfare you do not fight just to prevail in an argument, but to destroy the enemy's fighting ability. Republicans often seem to regard political combats as they would debates before the Oxford Political Union, as though winning depended on rational arguments and carefully articulated principles. But the audience of politics is not made up of Oxford dons, and the rules are entirely different.

You have only thirty seconds to make your point. Even if you had time to develop an argument, the audience you need to reach (the undecided and those in the middle who are not paying much attention) wouldn't get it. Your words would go over some of their heads and the rest would not even hear them (or would quickly forget) amid the bustle and pressure of daily life. Worse, while you've been making your argument, the other side has already painted you as a mean-spirited borderline racist controlled by religious zealots, securely in the pockets of the rich. Nobody who sees you this way is going to listen to you in any case. You're politically dead. Politics is war; don't forget it.

2. POLITICS IS A WAR OF POSITION

In war there are two sides: friends and enemies. Your task is to define yourself as the friend of as large a constituency as possible compatible with your principles, while defining your opponent as the enemy whenever you can. The act of defining combatants is analogous to the military concept of choosing the terrain of battle. Choose the ground that makes the fight as easy for you as possible. But be careful. American politics takes place in a pluralistic framework, where constituencies are diverse and often in conflict. "Fairness" and "tolerance" are the formal rules of democratic engagement. If you appear mean spirited or too judgmental, your opponent will more easily define you as a threat, and therefore as "the enemy" (see principle 4).

3. IN POLITICAL WARFARE, THE AGGRESSOR USUALLY PREVAILS

Republicans often pursue a conservative strategy of waiting for the other side to attack. In football, this is known as a "prevent defense." In politics, it is the strategy of losers.

Aggression is advantageous because politics is a war of position, which is defined by images that stick. By striking first, you can define the issues as well as your adversary. Defining the opposition is the decisive move in all political war. Other things being equal, whoever is on the defensive generally loses.

In attacking your opponent, take care to do it effectively. Politics is more *jiu-jitsu*-like than a slugfest. "Going negative" increases the risk of being defined as an enemy, and it can therefore be counterproductive. Ruling out the negative, however, can incur an even greater risk. In the 1998 California senatorial election, Barbara Boxer—one of the most left-wing Democrats (in fact, the number one spender in the entire Congress)—crushed a bland, moderate Republican. Matt Fong was so moderate he was able to get the endorsement of the leading liberal papers—the *Los Angeles Times* and the *San Francisco Chronicle*—and was running ahead in the polls. But Boxer went negative and Fong did not. As a result, the leftist was able to define herself as the moderate and the moderate as the extremist. The American public favors the center. The decision to avoid the negative did not save Fong from being defined by his opponent as mean spirited. But it did cost him the election. Never say "never" in political battles. It's an art, not a science.

4. POSITION IS DEFINED BY FEAR AND HOPE

The twin emotions of politics are fear and hope. Those who provide people with hope become their friends; those who inspire fear become enemies. Of the two, hope is the better choice. By offering people hope and yourself as its provider, you show your better side and maximize your potential support.

But fear is a powerful and indispensable weapon. If your opponent defines you negatively enough, he will diminish your ability to offer hope. That is why Democrats are so determined to portray Republicans as hostile to minorities, the middle class, and the poor.

The smear campaign against Clarence Thomas, for example, was designed to taint all black Republicans. It was a warning to other blacks who might stray from the Democratic fold. Without their captive black constituency—the most powerful symbol of their concern for the victimized—Democrats would be dead at the polls. They would lose every major urban center and become a permanent political minority. Democrats exploit their image as the party of blacks to stigmatize Republicans as the party of racists. The success of these tactics means that as a Republican you may have a lot to offer African Americans and other minorities, but you will have to work extra hard to get anyone to listen.

Liberals have successfully associated the Religious Right with moralistic intolerance. They have been helped by intolerant pronouncements from religious leaders and by groups with politically toxic names like the "Moral Majority" and "Christian Coalition." As a result, it is easy for liberals to portray them as a threat to any constituency that does not share their values: "They will impose their morals on you." It does not matter whether this is true or not. Once a negative image has taken hold, the target is wounded—often mortally—in the political battle.

To combat this form of attack, it is important to work away from the negative image your opponent wants to pin on you. If you know you are going to be attacked as morally imperious, it's a good idea to lead with a position that is inclusive and tolerant. If you are going to be framed as mean spirited and ungenerous, it is a good idea to put on a smile and lead with acts of generosity and charity. This will provide a shield from attack. When Clinton signed the welfare reform bill, he made sure he was flanked by two welfare mothers.

Symbols are so powerful that if you manipulate them cleverly, as Democrats do, you can even launch mean-spirited attacks on your opponents and pretend to be compassionate while doing it. Democrats understand, for example, that positioning themselves as victims gives them a license to attack. A gay politician like Barney Frank can assault an opponent and call it self-defense. Hillary Clinton can issue McCarthy-like proclamations about a "vast right wing conspiracy" and get away with it because she is a woman and because she has allies who will make her aggression look like self-defense. In the same way, Democrats rely on black extremists like Maxine Waters to slander Republicans as racists.

But remember this: Using fear as a weapon can be dangerous. Enemies inspire fear; friends do not. That is why the Clintons let their surrogates do the dirty work. When and how to use fear is a political art. If you are a white male in a culture whose symbols have been defined by liberals, be careful when you go on the offensive. Be sure to surround yourself with allies who are neither male nor white.

5. THE WEAPONS OF POLITICS
ARE SYMBOLS THAT EVOKE FEAR AND HOPE

The most important symbol is the candidate. Does the candidate inspire fear or hope? Voters want to know: Is the candidate someone who cares about people like me? Do I feel good about him, or does he put me on guard? Would I want to sit next to him at dinner?

Style, especially for high public office, is as important as any issue or strategy. Jack Kennedy—a relatively inexperienced, do-nothing congressman and senator—was able to win a national election merely by reciting problems and then repeating the litany "we can do bettah." Why? In part it was because he was handsome, witty, young, and charming—and wasn't a zealot.

Republicans lose a lot of political battles because they come across as hard edged, scolding, scowling, and sanctimonious. A good rule of thumb is to be just the opposite. You must convince people you care about them before they'll care about what you have to say. When you speak, don't forget that a sound bite is all you have. Whatever you have to say, make sure to say it loud and clear. Keep it simple and keep it short—a slogan is always better. Repeat it often. Put it on television. In politics, television is reality.

Of course, you have a base of supporters who will listen for hours to what you have to say. In the battles facing you, they will play an important role. What you say to them, therefore, is also important. But it is not going to decide elections. The audiences that will determine your fate are audiences that you will first have to persuade. You will have to find a way to reach them, get them to listen, and then to support you. With these audiences, you will never have time for real arguments or proper analyses. Images—symbols and sound bites—will always prevail. It is absolutely essential, therefore, to focus your message and repeat it over and over again. For a candidate this means the strictest discipline. Lack of focus will derail your message. If you make too many points, your message will be diffused and nothing will get through. The result will be the same as if you had made no point at all.

The same is true for the party as a whole. Democrats have a party line. When they are fighting an issue, they focus their agenda. Every time a Democrat steps in front of the cameras, there is at least one line in his speech that is shared with his colleagues. "Tax breaks for the wealthy at the expense of the poor" is one example. Repetition ensures that the message will get through. When Republicans speak, they all march to a different drummer. There are many messages instead of one. One message is a sound bite. Many messages are a confusing noise.

Symbols and sound bites determine the vote. These are what hit people in the gut before they have time to think. And these are what people remember. Symbols are the impressions that last and therefore that ultimately define you. Carefully chosen words and phrases are more important than paragraphs, speeches, party platforms, and manifestos. What you project through images is what you are.

The faces that represent Republicans are also symbols of whom Republicans represent. In a pluralistic community, diversity is important. Currently, too many Republican faces (what you see on your television screen) are Southern white men.

America is based on the idea that individual merit is what counts. As defenders of American principles, conservatives reject artificial diversity and racial quotas. But this is political warfare. Images are what counts. The image is the medium, and the medium is the message. Diversity, therefore, is more than important. It is crucial to becoming a national majority. But it is also crucial because it is just.

6. VICTORY LIES ON THE SIDE OF THE PEOPLE

This is the bottom line for each of the principles and for all of the principles. You must define yourself in ways that people understand. You must give people hope in your victory and make them fear the victory of your opponent. You can accomplish both by identifying yourself and your issues with the underdog and the victim, with minorities and the disadvantaged, with the ordinary Janes and Joes.

This is what Democrats do best and Republicans often neglect to do at all. Every political statement by a Democrat is an effort to say: "Democrats care about women, children, minorities, working Americans, and the poor. Republicans are mean spirited, serve the rich, and don't care about you." This is the Democrats' strategy of political war. If Republicans are to win the political war and become a national majority, they have to turn these images around.

They also have to make their campaigns a cause. During the Cold War, Republicans had a cause. They were saving the country from communism and—in its later decades—from leftist appeasers. The cause resonated at every level with the American people. The poorest citizens understood that their freedom was at stake in electing Republicans to conduct the nation's defense.

In a democracy, the cause that fires up passions is the cause of the people. That is why politicians like to run "against Washington" and against anything that represents the "powers that be." As the Left has shown, the idea of justice is a powerful motivator. It will energize the troops and fuel the campaigns that are necessary to win the political war. Republicans believe in economic opportunity and individual freedom.

The core of their ideas is justice for all. If they could make this intelligible to the American electorate, they would make themselves the party of the American people.

THE PRACTICE

Those are the principles. Here are some examples of the ways they work (and do not work).

TRUTH IN LABELING

"Tax breaks for the wealthy on the backs of the poor" is the Democratic sound bite that defines Republicans as mean-spirited fat cats and enemies of the poor. It is a lie that has been imprinted on the electorate through a million repetitions. It is the chant of every Democrat in Congress and every Democratic pundit. What is the Republican chant? There is none.

The first new weapon Republicans need in their arsenal is a sound bite that defines the Democrats and neutralizes this attack. The Democrat slogan is effective because it applies all the principles: It is not an argument that can be refuted; it is an *image* that imprints itself on the mind as a self-evident whole. It defines Republicans as enemies of the people. It doesn't have to be defended, because it doesn't bother to justify itself.

An image or sound bite is the crucial form of political firepower. It is a voter-seeking missile. If amplified by television or radio, it is like a cruise missile that can go thousands of miles to hit an individual target dead center. Think of yourself as separated from the electorate by oceans of static. Local and international news, family matters, work demands, business affairs, entertainment, and other distractions all clutter the airwaves between you and the voters. The sound bite, like a cruise missile, gets through. That's what makes it decisive.

Neither counterargument nor reason can combat the Democrats' class-warfare missile. The people the Democrats' sound bite reaches will never hear the counterargument or the evidence that refutes the Democratic smear. The static is too great; the clutter is too dense. Never underestimate the difficulty of reaching the people with a political message. The only effective response to a sound bite is another sound bite, a political cruise missile.

Here is a suggestion for the Republican sound bite: "Taxes for bureaucrats out of the pockets of the people."

This is an answer to the Democrats. Nothing longer will do the job. "Taxes for bureaucrats out of the pockets of the people" sums up what Democratic policies are all about. If the trillions spent by the welfare state went to poor people instead of to bureaucrats, there would be no poor people. If the billions spent on education went to the classroom and paid teachers to teach (instead of merely show up for the job), there would be no education crisis.

The sound bite principle can be applied to other political issues as well. Republicans should label their bills with language that gives them an advantage. Unfortunately, Republicans don't pay enough attention to details like this. Take their "Education Savings Bill," which failed to pass in the 1998 legislative session. Its very name projects an image of frugality that fits the Democrats' negative image of Republicans as mean-spirited accountants. "Education Savings Bill" sounds stingy: "Let's spend less on education." In naming their bill, Republicans did the Democrats' work for them. They reinforced a negative image and made themselves targets even before the Democrats got around to attacking them as supporters of a "tax break for the wealthy on the backs of the poor."

Wealthy people, of course, don't need a tax break to send their children to private schools. Working Americans do. So why not say so? Why not call this legislation the "Working Americans Education Bill"? And why not remind voters every chance you get that it's well-heeled Democratic legislators who send their own kids to private schools while denying working Americans and the poor the same privilege. Republicans complain that Democrats use the politics of "class warfare" against them, but Democrats will use class warfare as long as it works. The only way to stop them is to turn it around. *Taxes for bureaucrats out of the pockets of the people.* "The Democrats' policies mean private schools for the liberal elites and educational squalor for working Americans." *That's* a voter-seeking missile.

Issues and bills are not the only things that can be labeled to positive effect. Individuals and parties can as well. Of course, it is difficult to label a whole party, so Democrats seize on a radical wing of the Republican Party and say that the party itself is a captive of its extreme elements. The "Christian Right" has been demonized by liberal activists and has become a symbol of intolerance, zealotry, and hostility to minorities. Liberals then use the Christian Right to demonize the Republican Party as a whole.

Typically the Republican response to such attacks is tentative and defensive—"I am not an extremist"—and thus doomed to failure. Democrats label Republicans "right wing," meaning "intolerant, extreme." It is difficult if not impossible to disprove a negative. While you are busy defending yourself, the opposition is on the attack. That's why the best defense is always an offense. But instead of calling Democrats "left wing" and "radical," Republicans call Democrats "liberals," as though they were fair minded and generous, and open to new ideas. They are not. You cannot have an offense unless you are armed, and Republicans have no corresponding stigma to apply to Democrats.

Is this because the Democratic Party has no radical wing? Hardly. There is a socialist wing of the Democratic coalition in the Congressional Progressive Caucus, whose politics are indistinguishable from those of the radical Left.[2] Dozens of congressional Democrats have identified themselves as members of this caucus, which is formally allied with the Democratic Socialists of America and other radical organizations.[3] During the Clinton years, forty members of the Congressional Black Caucus made a "sacred covenant" with America's leading racist and Jew-hater, Louis Farrakhan,[4] but Republicans made nothing of this at the time, and it is now forgotten. On the other hand, one speaking engagement by a Republican congressman to an obscure "Conservative Citizens Council," associated in name and some personnel with the long-defunct White Citizens Councils, can be effectively exploited by Democrats to tar Republicans and accuse them of consorting with racists.

Government unions that represent teachers and public employees are not only living conflicts of interest (special interests that elect their own employers and lobby to raise their own salaries). They are also the socialist vanguards of the Democratic Party, whose only consistent agenda is to expand the state.

Here are better labels for Democrats than "liberals"—*leftists* and *radicals*. Republicans should practice referring to Democrats like Maxine Waters as "my opponent from the Far Left," and to "my left-wing colleagues Bernie Sanders and Barney Frank." They should stop blaming the media for describing leftists as "liberals," while letting them off the hook themselves.

WINNING WITH A LOSING ISSUE

With the right strategy, you can even win an election with a "third-rail" issue in a losing state. The November 1998 elections in California were an unmitigated disaster for the Republican Party, a defeat unparalleled in the state since the 1930s. The Republican gubernatorial candidate lost to his opponent by twenty points, taking down virtually the entire slate.

The results in the Hispanic community were even worse. Hispanic mistrust of Republicans deepened over two elections as a result of anti–illegal immigrant ballot initiatives. So deep was the alienation that the Republican gubernatorial candidate got only 17 percent to 23 percent of the Hispanic vote, depending on the exit poll, in 1998. The disastrous showing occurred even though the Republican campaign was better financed than the Democrat opposition and ran more Hispanic candidates than the Democrats did. The Republican gubernatorial candidate, moreover, made an extra effort in the Hispanic community, including a television ad campaign on Spanish-language television.

Five months earlier, however, in the same state, the results of a Republican ballot initiative on a hot-button Hispanic issue were exactly the reverse. The initiative to end bilingual education was denounced by every major newspaper and establishment figure in California, by the chairmen of both the Republican and Democratic parties, and by the Republican candidate for governor. The anti-bilingual campaign was able to raise only 1.5 million dollars and could not finance a single television ad, while the opposition spent 4.8 million dollars and financed a strong television advertising campaign.

Despite these enormous obstacles, the anti-bilingual campaign won a landslide victory, with 61 percent voting for it and only 39 percent against. It also received 35 percent of the Hispanic vote—twice what the Republican gubernatorial candidate would receive five months later.

How could this happen? The answer is that the sponsors of the anti-bilingual initiative followed the principles of political war, especially the most basic: positioning yourself on the side of the people. They defined themselves as friends of Hispanic children who were trying to learn English and better their lives. This won the sympathy and support not only of Hispanics who wanted their children to have a chance in life, but of all those who saw immigrant children as society's underdogs deserving a fair shake.

At their first press conference, the sponsors said they were responding to a recent demonstration by Hispanic parents demanding that their children be taught in English, a privilege that the existing bilingual programs—which were programs taught in Spanish—denied them. Among the sponsors were a Hispanic teacher-activist and an Episcopal nun who had run her own program to teach English to poor Hispanic children.

There were many arguments that could have been made for teaching Hispanic immigrants English. Bilingualism could reasonably be seen as a threat to national unity. Canada is a ready-to-hand example of what can happen to a country with more than one official language. But such a positioning of the initiative would have invited the response that it was anti-immigrant and would persecute a vulnerable segment of the community. This would have played into the hands of the left-wing opposition and would have made it easy for them to portray the sponsors as enemies of children, minorities, and the poor. Positioned that way, the initiative would have failed.

But once the anti-bilingual initiative was presented as a helping hand to a disadvantaged group, victory was assured. Early polls taken before the opposition was able to mount its smear campaign showed the initiative winning 80 percent overall and 83 percent of Hispanic voters. Not even a $4.8 million campaign smearing its proponents as "xenophobes" and "racists" could whittle that figure to below 60 percent. This is what a strategically sound position on the battlefield can accomplish.

COMPASSIONATE CONSERVATISM

When Democrats speak, every other word is "women," "children," "minorities," "working Americans," or "the poor." This immediately organizes the battlefield in a way that favors their victory. All Americans regard themselves as underdogs. Most are tolerant and compassionate. Concern for minorities and the vulnerable resonates with Americans' sense of their better selves. Going into political battle, you want to be on the side of the angels.

The Democrats' rhetoric speaks directly to the American people about things they understand—the concrete lives of their fellow human beings. Speaking about women, children, minorities, working Americans, and the poor makes the connection. It establishes a link between speaker and listener. It appears to come from the heart. If it comes across sincerely, it immediately identifies the speaker as a friend.

Republicans, by contrast, tend to speak in abstract language about legalistic doctrines and economic budgets. They sound like businessmen, lawyers, and accountants. They argue the virtues of flat taxes versus value-added taxes. They talk about capital gains tax cuts. They speak from the head instead of the heart. But most Americans do not know what capital is, let alone a capital gain. If you had an hour (instead of thirty seconds) and were able to explain to them why a capital gains tax might be a double tax, it would probably make no difference at all. When you were finished, most of them would shrug their shoulders and say, "They're rich enough, let them pay it anyway." Whatever their conclusions, they would certainly not feel especially close to Republicans in the end.

Bill Clinton entered the budget negotiations in the fall of 1998 as a wounded president and a figure of national disgust. But his political strategy was classic Democratic warfare: He positioned himself as a defender of the weak; he positioned his opponents as uncaring advocates of the greedy and the strong.

"We have a budget surplus for the first time in a generation," Clinton might have said. "Let's show that we care. Let's give a billion dollars to the children. Better yet, so that everybody will notice our caring, let's break the budget cap. Let's just add it to the education package already in the bill." His real message was this: "However bad I may be, I'm still the only hope the children have against these mean-spirited Republicans who will deny their needs." It was a winning strategy, but for it to work politically, Republicans had to play their familiar role as the bad hats, the Scrooges who would say, "We don't have the money."

Republicans knew, of course, that not much of Clinton's education money would reach any children. It would go into the coffers of the education bureaucracy and the teacher unions, whose members get paid not for how well they teach but just for showing up. In short, Clinton's plan was *tax money for bureaucrats out of the pockets of the people.* But even this sound bite, had the Republicans used it, would have been trumped by the sound bite Clinton was counting on: "Democrats want more money for education; the Republicans want less." And that's the way it would be played. There would be no public debate. There would be only this sound bite in the morning papers and on the evening news: "President Proposes More Money for Education. Republicans Call for Less." If Republicans refused to agree to more money, they were going to lose.

So what did the Republicans do? At least they were clever enough not to say, "There's no money." That was a bad answer that would have cost them dearly. Instead they responded, "Where's the money?"—as though Clinton would have to answer. It was a marginal improvement, but the result was exactly the same.

It's easy to come up with a response for Clinton: "C'mon! It's a five-hundred-billion-dollar bill we're talking about. You mean there's not an *eentsy, beentsy* billion for the children?" There is no winning answer to that question. There is no answer at all. Republicans realized this within a few hours, conceded the inevitable, and signed off on the bill. Politically, it was a typical Republican performance: They managed to look mean spirited, stupid, and weak, all at same time.

What could they have done to prevent this defeat? They could have positioned themselves on the side of the children and defined their Democratic opponents as enemies of the children. They could have said, "We want ten billion dollars for the children, not a measly one billion. But we want it in the form of scholarships for the inner-city kids you Democrats have trapped in failing and dangerous public schools." This would have rammed Clinton up against the teachers' unions, the largest special interest in the Democratic Party and the chief opponent of school reforms. It would have positioned Republicans as the advocates of the most disadvantaged, oppressed, and deprived of America's children. This would have exposed the Democrats (who send their own children to private schools) as hypocritical oppressors of minorities and the poor.

Why is it that no Republican ever reminds people that Democrats and liberals have controlled every major urban school system in the nation for more than sixty years? If there is a national education crisis, Democrats and progressives are responsible. Why should Bill Clinton, Ted Kennedy, and Jesse Jackson be able to send their children to private schools while preventing inner-city parents from having the same privilege and choice?

If the disastrous condition of our schools has blighted the lives of millions upon millions of poor and minority children, Democrats and progressives are responsible. If education is the crucial ladder of immigrant success, Democrats have denied millions of immigrant children the use of that ladder. By creating a paternalistic system that does not serve the poorest and neediest segments of society, by inflicting tax burdens and regulations that limit economic opportunity, Democrats and progressives have severely restricted opportunities for minorities and the poor. Republicans have a solution. They intend to revive those opportunities, to liberate minorities through educational choice, through policies that restore the bottom rungs of the ladder of success. That is the message Republicans need to take to the American people.

The Republican Party can be a majority party, but only if it respects the common sense of the American people, recovers Ronald Reagan's optimism ("It's morning in America"), diversifies the face it presents to the voting public, remembers that policies affect real live people, and never forgets that the American electorate is very large and (when it comes to politics) hard of hearing. Above all, Republicans need to remember their heritage as the party of Lincoln, of principle, of the underdog—as the party of the American dream.

CHAPTER NINE

HOW TO BEAT THE DEMOCRATS

This was originally published, in pamphlet form, in 2000.

Politics is war conducted by other means. If you didn't understand this before the Democrats tried to overturn the 2000 presidential election result in Florida, you probably do now. It doesn't matter whether you think such behavior is proper. It doesn't matter whether you like it or not. If you don't come to the arena ready to fight a political war, the Democrats will. And they will win.

To win in war, you need to know your enemy, which means you need to answer these questions: Who is he? What motivates him? What are his strengths and weaknesses? What is he capable of?

The time to start thinking about the next election is now. It doesn't matter whether the vote is next month or next year. It doesn't matter whether it's a year away or four. Start preparing now. Because *the Democrats already are.*

For Democrats, politics is a permanent war. Every conflict is a contest for power; every battle is about burying their enemies. About burying *you.* Not just in this election, but in the next. That's what half the battle in Florida was about. If the Democrats couldn't win by overturning the result, they could damage the winner through a political brawl. "Among…pragmatic elected officials, especially members of Congress," observed the *Wall Street Journal,* "it's about tarnishing a Bush presidency and preparing for 2002."[1]

For Democrats, politics is not just about who's in office, or which policy will prevail. If it were, Democrats would not be so ruthless in their pursuit of victory. But for them, the political war is about matters of even greater moment. It's about good and evil. It's about control over the future. It's about changing the world. These ends will justify almost any means. That's why Florida in 2000 should have been a wake-up call for Republicans.

Most Republicans do not share Democrats' attitude toward the political process (and, of course, neither do some moderate Democrats). Republicans think of politics as a way to fix government so that it will work better. They want to preserve the core principles of the Founding Fathers. These are important goals, but they are not as ambitious as their opponents' schemes.

More important, Republicans' very pragmatism leads them to believe that sometimes it might be better to lose than to persist in a political conflict that would hurt the country. Republicans pressed their own president to step down after Watergate. They were willing to injure their own cause in order to do what they thought was right.

Democrats rarely exhibit such scruples, as their win-at-any-cost tactics in Florida showed. Their goals—fighting "evil" and changing the world—are too important, their hunger for power too strong, to permit such political restraint. As Florida demonstrated, many Democrats feel morally obliged not only to win elections but to steal them if that's what it takes to make a "better world."[2]

Because Democrats feel the need for power so strongly, they involve themselves in the political battle all day, every day. They are ready to give up normal lives for the privilege of waging the political war. For Democrats, politics is not just about *who* will run the government. It's about the nature of government itself.

For example, Democrats regard the Constitution as a "living" document, that is, one that can be altered at will. The Constitution for them is an outdated arrangement that obstructs their progressive schemes. That is the real meaning of "liberal" court decisions on abortion, prayer, gender relations, crime, punishment, and other matters crucial to the nation's cultural life. Those courts were no more "liberal" than the Democrats themselves. "Radical" is the term that describes what they did.

For Democrats, politics is not about adjusting the framework the Founders devised. It's about inventing a new America—a nation governed by racial and gender preferences, economic entitlements and executive orders; a nation in which property rights are diminished and citizens become subjects of a cradle-to-grave, we-know-what-is-good-for-you guardian state. For Democrats, politics is really about who gets to define the American future.

That's why Republicans must recognize that political war is a life-and-death struggle for the America they love. If you love what the Founders created, start fighting now.

THE IDEA IS TO WIN

Politics is about winning. It seems obvious, but Republicans sometimes forget it. Many seem to think that politics is only about being right: if you espouse good principles and proclaim good policies, you've performed your political task. In one sense, of course, politics *is* about such things. Why engage in political battles if you don't think you are wiser or more principled than your opponent? But politics is also a war in which almost anything goes. Consequently, good principles and good policies go down to defeat as often as not.

Every good citizen would like elections to be about issues and not about personalities or catchy sound bites. But real-world elections almost never are. The public is not willing to pay the necessary attention. If it were, policy debates would be prime-time television events like game shows and sports. But even then, the public would wander in the political dark. That's because politicians and their hired consultants work hard to confuse voters and misrepresent their opponents' case. In an ideal world, it wouldn't be that way. But in this one, it is.

Those who think they can win elections on superior principles and better issues are what I call "Gold Star" Republicans. Gold Star Republicans believe that if they show voters they are decent human beings and support good policies, they will be rewarded. But that's not the way the political war works. Just look at what Democrats did to Clarence Thomas and Robert Bork, whose careers were exemplary before the Left went after them. The politics of personal destruction was also on display in the 2000 election. When Democrats weren't defaming George Bush as a mental midget, they were running a multimillion-dollar scare campaign to warn seniors he would bankrupt the Social Security system and take away their pensions.

The NAACP conducted its own multimillion-dollar ad campaign featuring the daughter of a lynching victim who said she felt George Bush had killed her father "a second time," because he did not support her position on "hate crimes" legislation. It was shameful. Democrats smeared Bush as a coldhearted racist who would not protect African Americans against a lynch mob if he were elected president. They did this to a man whose public record was above reproach, a governor who took special pride in having raised the education levels of African American children in his state. Bush ran a campaign of "compassionate conservatism" and went out of his way to reach out to African Americans. But the Democrats tarred him as a "racist" indifferent to minority concerns. Over 90 percent of African American voters bought some or all of the Democrats' lies.

Political war is unfair, and you don't get to make the rules. When your opponents are Democrats, hate campaigns are what you can expect. If Democrats don't use gutter tactics to defeat you, it will be because they think they can beat you without them.[3]

To win against Democrats, you don't have to stoop to their shameful level or adopt their disgraceful tactics. But you *do* have to know what you are up against. And you'd better have a plan to fight back.

Politics is not the same as policy, nor is it the same as acting on principle. Politics is about getting the power to *implement* policy and put principles into *practice*. These are the iron rules: you don't get to make policy or put your principles into practice if you don't win the political war.

Politics *is* about winning the war. If you are not focused on winning, you are in the wrong business. Go look for something else to do—become a preacher or a missionary. Do charity work. Write books.

FOUR PRINCIPLES OF POLITICS

In order to win the political war, it is necessary to understand its basic principles.

1. POLITICS IS A WAR OF EMOTIONS

For the great mass of the public, casting a vote is not an intellectual choice but a gut decision. It is based on impressions that may be superficial and premises that could be misguided. The art of political war is about evoking emotions that favor one's goals. It is the ability to manipulate the public's feelings in support of your agenda while arousing fear of your opponent. George W. Bush is a decent man. There is nothing farther from his heart than the hateful act of a racial lynching. He would never dream of taking away old people's pensions. Yet the Democrats persuaded millions of voters to believe just that, and they voted against him.

2. POLITICS IS A WAR OF POSITION

If a majority of the electorate perceives your party to be the party of the people—if you position yourself on their side—you will win. But the same rule holds whether you actually serve their interests or not. It all depends on how you play it.

Just consider all those black and Hispanic children whose parents voted for Democrats but who are trapped in failing government schools that Democrats control. Just think of the inner city with its crumbling housing, dangerous streets, rampaging drug gangs, moral breakdown, and economic decay. In every such community, Democrats control the city council, the elected school board, and the administrative agencies. Democrats have shaped the life of America's inner cities for more than half a century. Insofar as Democrats offer policies for the inner cities, they are failed policies. Insofar as they have principles to guide their policies, they are the wrong principles. Yet Democrats invariably win between 80 and 90 percent of the inner-city vote. That's what shrewd political positioning can achieve.

The art of politics is about getting a majority of voters to identify with you in their gut. To win, it helps if you have good principles and good policies. But having a good image for yourself and attaching a bad image to your opponent is even better.

3. FEAR IS A POLITICAL WEAPON

To win in politics, you must convince a majority of the voters that you are their friend. But almost as important, you must get them to *fear* your opponent as their enemy. "I will fight for you," was Al Gore's battle cry in the election; "I will fight *them*." Who is "them"? The answer is the corporate interests. The answer is the rich and powerful. The answer is the Republican Party, which the Democrats identify as the party of corporate interests and of the rich and powerful.

No matter how much Republicans deplore such tactics, no matter how fervently they wish that electoral contests would turn on good policies and good principles, it is not in their power to change the reality of political war. Anger, fear, and resentment are among the most potent weapons in the Democrats' arsenal: resentment of success; anger at the Grinches who cheat the poor and steal old folks' pensions; fear of bigots and lynchers. These are powerful myths that drive voters to the polls to pull the Democratic lever. If they are not countered, these emotions will bury the Gold Stars every time.

When Al Gore was lagging in the presidential race, Democratic leaders said they were not concerned. They said they would "win on the issues." Now that the race is over, even the most complacent Gold Star Republican can see what these Democrats meant. They meant that they would use the issues to distort what Republicans stood for and make the voters fear them.

In the Democrats' hands, the issues would become political weapons. They would use the issues to smear Republicans by any means necessary.

As Election Day approached, the Democrats made "hate crimes" a major campaign point. To Republicans, the "hate crimes" issue was a policy debate about the constitutionality of defining "thought crimes." For Democrats, it was a chance to *commit* a hate crime against Republicans. It was an opportunity to burn the image of a Texas lynching into the psyches of American minorities and make them fear Republicans everywhere.

After the ads had done their work, 92 percent of all African Americans voted against George Bush. This was more African Americans than had voted against Ronald Reagan or Bob Dole or Richard Nixon. And none of these men had made half the effort George W. Bush had to woo the African American vote.

Democrats get away with such tactics because they are adept at the war of position. By using minorities to launch the race-baiting attacks, Democrats are able to frame Republicans so that they appear to be against minorities, and Democrats appear to be their friends.

4. POLITICS IS ABOUT HOPE

Seeking to win the political center may seem counter to the spirit of political war, but it is really its main idea: to make the Republican Party the party of the majority of the people. The key to the center is hope.

The American people want their leaders to be tough minded but inclusive; disciplined but tolerant; responsible but also caring. That is why in 1996 they elected Bill Clinton on a Republican platform—balanced budgets and welfare reform. They thought of him as a Republican with a heart. They wanted a leader who would impose limits and restraints, but who was also sensitive to their needs. It was the same calculation that enabled George Bush to run neck and neck, as a "compassionate" Republican, in an election Democrats should have won in a landslide.

Politics may be a war zone, but the winning emotion is still hope. Victorious candidates persuade voters that they provide the best hope for a better future and a more united country. Fear may be an important weapon in neutralizing a negative campaign ("Al Gore will say anything to be president"), but hope is the emotion that inspires people and wins political elections ("I will leave no child behind").

While thinking about political war, it is extremely important to remember that independent and swing voters, who are the ultimate arbiters of elections, are not partisans, do not relate to politics as a political war, and can barely tell the difference between the parties—let alone the candidates. This is partly because American politics is not ideological in the European sense. But it is mainly because of the success of America itself.

The much-lamented fact that 50 percent of the eligible electorate do not vote at all reflects the great good fortune that most Americans enjoy in this land of opportunity. They are too busy getting on with the business of their lives to pay much attention to what looks to them like partisan squabbles. Americans want leaders who are uniters. They want politicians who offer them hope.

In short, political war is more complex than the real thing, beginning with the battleground itself. The public that decides its outcome does not like to think of it as "war" at all. They want their leaders to govern them rather than lead them in battle. Often they are not even paying enough attention to know if a battle is being fought on their behalf. They regard most politicians as interchangeable and available to the highest bidder.

The public's desires are often contradictory. They want their politicians to be "for" them, but they don't want them to be "partisan." They want government programs that benefit them, but they don't want higher taxes. Consequently, there are many times when the political battle assumes the aspect of a game of poker rather than a serious conflict. Politicians regularly mask their partisan intentions. "Flying below the radar" and conducting silent attacks are strategies in political war too.

If this seems confusing, here's a way to think about it: Ronald Reagan was a great Cold War leader. When he became president, his first moves in office were to rearm America and confront the Soviets with overwhelming firepower. While liberals denounced him as a warmonger, Reagan ignored their warnings and called his adversary an "evil empire." He stripped away the Soviets' moral credibility and diminished their political influence. Addressing their leader from a podium in front of the Berlin Wall, Reagan said, "Mr. Gorbachev, tear down this wall." But Reagan's next step was not martial at all. From a position of moral and military strength, he extended an olive branch to the isolated Gorbachev and gave him a great big bear hug. And the wall came tumbling down.

FIVE LESSONS OF THE 2000 ELECTION

LESSON 1: STRATEGY IS DECISIVE

In a year of economic boom and relative peace, against an administration that registered 60 percent approval ratings with the American public, the Republican victory was something like a political miracle. Academic political scientists, working with models based on the economic climate and presidential elections over the previous one hundred years, had predicted that Al Gore would win 55 percent of the popular vote. Al Gore won only 48 percent.[4]

This is the first lesson of the election campaign: political strategies are decisive. With the right political battle plan, you can win, even when the odds say you can't. It is an especially important lesson for Republicans, who are prone to pessimism. Low expectations are a feature of the conservative outlook. Conservatives are realists. They appreciate human weakness and understand how wishful thinking inspires the illusions that favor the Left. But because conservative expectations are low, they easily become self-fulfilling visions of defeat. Conservatives need to remind themselves that they too can make a difference. If the left-wing media and the Democratic Party had had their way during the Cold War, the Soviet empire would still be with us. Conservatives need to remember the victories they have won against the odds. They could do worse than adopt the motto of Antonio

Gramsci,[5] a famous strategist of the Left, who said a revolutionary must be guided by "pessimism of the intellect, but optimism of the will."

LESSON 2: UNITY IN BATTLE IS THE KEY TO VICTORY

In the election, only 1 percent of Republicans defected to Patrick J. Buchanan's candidacy, compared with 3 percent of Democrats who voted for Nader. Without this superior Republican unity, the Republican candidate would have lost.

All political campaigns are about forming and maintaining majority coalitions. The very diversity of the electorate means that the success of national campaigns depends on a united political front. For the Republican Party, achieving this unity is not easy. Its coalition embraces amazing diversity—conservatives and moderates, secularists and religionists, moral absolutists and agnostic libertarians—for which Republicans rarely get the credit they deserve.

During the Cold War, the Republican coalition was unified by the seriousness with which it took the Soviet threat. But the Cold War is over, and maintaining this unity is far more difficult. Republicans need to remind themselves that America's security is still at risk and that its constitutional order is threatened by a political Left whose values remain socialist and whose agenda is subversive.

LESSON 3: THERE IS NO NATURAL CONSERVATIVE MAJORITY

The bad news of the election of 2000 is that nearly half the American people voted for 285 new federal programs, billions in new taxes, and the largest budget expansion since Lyndon Johnson's Great Society. The Republican victory was barely achieved against a campaign that was badly run by a leader widely perceived to lack character and integrity. Al Gore was vice president of a corrupt and disgraced administration. He personally broke election laws, lied to federal investigators, and seemed compulsively unable to stay within range of the facts. Yet Al Gore won a plurality of the popular vote.

Nearly half the electorate voted for a Democratic Party that denigrated the military, fiercely defended racial discrimination ("to make up for historic injustices"), and believed the U.S. Constitution is an outdated and bigoted document that needs to be rewritten to accommodate the left-wing agenda.

In a speech to "energize" his African American base, Al Gore attacked George Bush for promising to appoint Supreme Court justices who would remain faithful to the constitutional text. Said Gore, "I often think of the strictly constructionist meaning that was applied when the Constitution was written, how some people were considered three-fifths of a human being."[6] This bogus and inflammatory statement was a standard canard of the political Left.[7] Gore's misleading reference was his contribution to the Democrats' efforts to smear the Republican candidate as a closet racist seeking to turn back the clock on civil rights.

This unpleasant lesson of the election is one that many Republicans do not want to hear. Days before the vote, two of the brightest editors at *National Review* criticized the strategy of "compassionate conservatism" with which Bush had challenged Gore in his bid for the political center: "If Mr. Bush wins, it will not be because of his personality, compassionate or otherwise. It will be because America remains, in crucial respects, a conservative country that wants energetic conservative leaders."[8] This can hardly be the case in the sense the authors seem to imply. Al Gore ran a campaign well to the left of the American political center—too *far* to the left according to centrist critics in his own party. If Americans were conservative in the authors' sense, they would have roundly rejected Gore's populist appeal.

Such facts are no cause for conservatives to despair. What they are is a reality check. If the conservative mission is to restore basic American values, the *way* conservatives fight the political battle will determine its outcome. There may be no current conservative majority in America, but there is a potential majority, if Republicans have the will and intelligence to organize it.

LESSON 4: DEMOCRATS RELY ON BRIBERY AND FEAR

The eighteenth-century Scottish jurist and historian Alexander Tytler is said to have warned, "A democracy cannot exist as a permanent form of government. It can only exist until the voters discover that they can vote themselves money from the public treasury. From that moment on the majority always votes for the candidates promising the most money from the public treasury, with the result that a democracy always collapses over loose fiscal policy followed by a dictatorship."[9] The Democratic Party is aptly named in precisely this sense: it is a machine that runs on the corruption of the people.

Democrats' passion for big government is an expression of this corruption. Voters who look to government for entitlements look to the Democratic Party to supply them. Conversely, the Democrat Party recruits its supporters through taxpayer-funded programs that buy their votes.

Does this mean that Tytler was right and democracy is doomed? Only pessimists will surrender to the thought. Others will recognize three barriers to this undesirable outcome:

(1) The individualism of the American people, who have already withstood a thirty-year assault on the American identity and the American idea. Despite the Left's attacks on America as a racist, patriarchal, imperial oppressor, enough citizens still believe in individual rights, limited government, and the market system to have kept the country resilient and free.

(2) The impractical nature of the programs Democrats seek to expand. In the long run, big-government entitlements do not work, because there are few limits to what people think they deserve and even fewer to what they think they need. Such socialist schemes generally make no allowance for individual accountability and provide no incentives to individuals to create and produce. That is why impending bankruptcy—financial and moral—is their normal state.

(3) The Republican Party. Just because big government works badly or does not work at all will not discourage Democrats from pursuing an agenda that feeds their hunger for power and funds their political machine.

That is why the third and most important barrier to their designs is the Republican Party itself.

The modern Republican Party is not the "Party of the Establishment," and it is not the "Party of the Rich," as Democrats claim. It is the Party of Reform, infused with middle-class energies and entrepreneurial values. It is conservative only in the sense that its core principles are inspired by the framework that the Founders devised.

Only by misrepresenting Republicans and distorting their message can Democrats maintain their grip on power. This is why Democrats more and more depend on scare tactics to advance their agenda. No one could have said it better than Bush did, at the Republican convention in Philadelphia: "[Al Gore] now leads the party of Franklin Delano Roosevelt. But the only thing he has to offer is fear itself."[10] When Democrats label Republicans racists and even "Nazis," it is not an intellectual claim they are making. It is an emotional hand grenade thrown in the direction of Republican bunkers. Their objective is to create an explosion so loud that ordinary voters can no longer hear what Republicans are saying or think clearly about conservative arguments and positions. The most important political task for Republicans is to neutralize these attacks.

LESSON 5: "COMPASSION" IS A WINNING VIRTUE

In the 2000 presidential race, Republicans unveiled a slogan to neutralize the Democrats' fear attacks. With his agenda of "compassionate conservatism," Bush achieved victory despite a vicious smear campaign and an unfavorable electoral terrain. By celebrating racial, ethnic, and gender inclusion at the Republican convention and by contesting the "caring" issues of Social Security, healthcare, and education, Bush was able to take away the Democrats' target, neutralize their advantage, and make decisive inroads into constituencies and states that Democrats traditionally have won. These additions to the conservative fold provided the margin of Republican victory in a year when conventional wisdom predicted a Democratic landslide.

Contesting the caring issues to win the center will be essential to Republicans even in years that are favorable to Republican victory. Since the New Deal (and except on matters of defense), Democrats have been a majority coalition. It is only because Democrats moved sharply to the left on foreign policy during the 1972 McGovern campaign that they consistently lost the White House until the end of the Cold War.[11] At the same time, they continued to prevail on domestic issues, achieving decisive majorities in Congress virtually every year.

To win a national election, it is necessary to capture a majority among independents who occupy the political middle. It doesn't matter what Republicans call their strategy to achieve this outcome—"compassionate conservatism" or something else. For Republicans to win, it is necessary to compete with Democrats on the caring issues, to reach beyond the partisan core and expand the conservative base.

WHO THE DEMOCRATS ARE

The first thing to realize about the Democratic Party is that this is no longer the party of Harry Truman. As Patrick Caddell, a seasoned pollster, put it, "I'm a liberal Democrat. I started in Florida politics. I worked for George McGovern. I worked for Jimmy Carter. I've worked for Ted Kennedy, Mario Cuomo. Nobody can question, I think, my credentials and my convictions. But I have to tell you,…my party, the party that [my family has] belonged to since my great-great-grandfather…has become no longer a party of principles, but has been hijacked by a confederacy of gangsters who need to take power by whatever means and whatever canards they can."[12]

Consider the following marker: The politics of John F. Kennedy are not really different from the politics of Ronald Reagan. Kennedy was a militant anti-Communist and a hawk on defense, authorizing the biggest expansion of the military since World War II. He was in favor of a balanced budget and a capital-gains tax cut, and half of his cabinet—including his secretaries of state, Treasury, and defense—were Republicans. If Kennedy were alive today and held the same political views, the national media would describe him as "right-wing."

This is an indication of how far the Democratic Party has shifted to the left since the 1960s. It is true that Clinton's "New Democrat" strategy temporarily pushed the party toward the center. But as the history of the party since 2000 shows, without a leader as devious or adroit as Clinton, it will be difficult for this center to hold. The Democratic Party core remains solidly left and almost indistinguishable in outlook from the socialist parties of Europe.[13]

The Democrats' left-wing orientation has deep organizational roots. The party apparatus feeds off the entitlements of the welfare state: social workers, university intellectuals, trial lawyers, bureaucrats, and government unions are all clients of the big-government programs the party promotes. As Cleta Mitchell, an ex-Democrat, observed in the *Wall Street Journal*, her former party is Alexander Tytler's cynical vision come true: "The fundamental motivation for Democrats is their understanding that winning control of government is tied to paychecks, jobs, government grants, public money for private groups and companies, government contracts, union bargaining advantages, rules by which trial lawyers bring lawsuits.... The use of government to feed friends and starve enemies is something Democrats know instinctively. Winning elections means getting or keeping a livelihood. Say what you will about trial lawyers, but remember this: They only get paid if their clients win."[14]

To the mix of Boss Tweed operators and patronage pols must be added the progressive missionaries who make up the party's trade union, environmental, and "civil rights" Left. These are disciples of the old Communist religions who believe that government power can be used to redeem the world. They are convinced that government policies can reform smokers, rehabilitate criminals, vanquish racists, eliminate poverty, conquer "sexism," and create a world in which there will be no internal combustion engines, handguns, or wars. In Hillary Clinton's revealing words, the task of politics is nothing less than "to remold society by redefining what it means to be a human being in the twenty-first century...."[15]

It is well known that the constituencies of the Democratic Party are more conservative than the party's activists. Delegates to Democratic conventions (about a quarter of them from government unions) poll well to the left of Democrat voters. This offers Republicans an opportunity to make inroads into the Democrat base.

On the battlefield, however, it is the political Left that provides the party with the manpower of its political ground war and the firepower of its political air war.[16] Its search-and-destroy teams accuse Republicans of racism and sexism, of polluting the environment, and of abusing old people, women, and little children.

Marxism may be dead, but a Marxist moral imagination provides the ordnance for the Democrats' political attacks. The rhetorical artillery of class, race, and gender warfare puts Republicans on the defensive and pins their forces down. Unless this attack from the Left can be blunted, Democrats will continue to have the advantage going into combat.

In an article written during the Florida fracas, the Clinton strategist and Gore advisor Paul Begala revealed the inner thoughts of the Democrats' strike force:

> Yes...tens of millions of good people in Middle America voted Republican. But if you look closely at that [electoral] map [showing counties that voted Republican in red] you see a more complex picture. You see the state where James Byrd was lynch-dragged behind a pickup truck until his body came apart—it's red. You see the state where Matthew Shepard was crucified on a split-rail fence for the crime of being gay—it's red.[17] You see the state where right-wing extremists blew up a federal office building and murdered scores of federal employees—it's red. The state where an army private who was thought to be gay was bludgeoned to death with a baseball bat, and the state where

neo-Nazi skin-heads murdered two African Americans because of their skin color, and the state where Bob Jones University spews its anti-Catholic bigotry: they're all red too.[18]

This is the image of Republicans that Democratic spear carriers hold in their hearts: *Republicans are racists and lynchers.* Republicans should study Begala's diatribe, because it offers a glimpse of the sniper on the other end of the gun that is always pointed at them. One could employ Begala's own style of political geography against him: The state where Muslim terrorists blew up the World Trade Center—that's blue. The county where a race riot following a court verdict destroyed two thousand Korean businesses and caused the deaths of fifty-eight people—that's blue, too. The states where Colin Ferguson and Ronald Taylor killed eight whites and Asians because left-wing race baiters convinced them they were victims of a racial conspiracy—true blue.[19] The counties, nationwide, where the vast majority of murderers, rapists, and child molesters live and operate—those are blue, too.

But more important than such a retort is to understand what Begala's outburst reveals about the Left. The passions that motivate them are self-righteousness and hate. They hate conservatives and Republicans, and think they are evil. Bill Clinton told Dick Morris exactly that. In the 1996 campaign he said, "Bob Dole is evil. The things he wants to do to children are evil. The things he wants to do to poor people and old people and sick people are evil. Let's get that straight."[20] Bob Dole is a war hero. In his career as majority leader of the Senate, he was a gentleman dealmaker. Yet to Clinton, Bob Dole is "evil." George Stephanopoulos's White House memoir recalls a similar episode in the Oval Office when Clinton was reminding him that congressional elections were coming and they needed to get back on the campaign trail. What Clinton said was: "It's Nazi time out there. We've got to hit them back."[21]

Republicans are often surprised when Democrats refer to them as "Nazis" and "fascists,"[22] the way Representative John Lewis did, for example,

on the floor of the House during a Medicare debate, or when they accuse
Republicans of taking food out of the mouths of children. When attacked
in these extreme terms, Republicans often become defensive. They worry
about whether it was something they said (or perhaps did) to elicit such
irrational suspicion and abuse. Republicans think, "If only we were more
careful.... If only we presented ourselves better." It's fine for Republicans to
put on their best face in public. That's the face that will persuade those in
the middle who are not ideological and whose votes decide elections. But
for the leftists who are the hard core of the Democratic Party, *nothing*
Republicans can do will stop them from thinking of Republicans as racists
and lynchers or from wanting them politically dead.

If you doubt this, look at what Democrats did to Clarence Thomas.
When he was nominated to a seat on the Supreme Court, Thomas had been
an upstanding citizen and civil servant for twenty years. He had risen from
circumstances of great adversity without a single blemish on his public
record. But this meant nothing to the Democrats. They went straight for
his jugular.

They employed the pretext that, in a private conversation ten years
before, he had allegedly used improper language with Anita Hill, *a Yale-
trained civil rights lawyer*. They said this was an outrage against a helpless
female who was unable to speak up for herself. They said that Thomas had
abused his position and power as her employer. They said by talking dirty
to her, he had committed a crime against all women. They called for his
head in the name of all women. Although they were unable to defeat his
nomination with these slanders, they succeeded in tarnishing his reputation
and neutralizing him as a public force.

A few years later, Bill Clinton had actual sex with a White House
employee. She was not an attorney with a degree from Yale with a portfolio
in civil rights law, but a confused college-aged intern. It was subsequently
revealed that Clinton had also groped a widow, demanded a sexual favor
from a state employee, and forced himself on a campaign worker. Unlike
Thomas, who never attacked the character of his accuser, Clinton and his

agents set out to destroy the reputations of each of his female victims when they came forward to speak about the abuse. Clinton even went so far as to lie in a court of law to accomplish this.

But when confronted with Clinton's sexual harassment, the same feminists, liberals, and progressives who had attempted the "high-tech lynching" of Thomas rushed to the president's defense. "He's just a man," they said. "Boys will be boys." Congressional Democrats who fancied themselves the social conscience of the nation were willing to go to the wall to keep a guilty male in power. "It's *only* sex," they said.

When the political chips were down, the Democrats' principles didn't matter. What mattered was that Clinton was one of them, and Clarence Thomas was not. And because he was not, they had to destroy him.

A WINNING STRATEGY

Democrats win elections because they understand a simple fact: the key to American politics is the romance of the underdog. Americans like the story of the little guy who goes up against the system and triumphs. It is a story about opportunity and fairness. To win the hearts and minds of the American voter, you have to tap the emotions it evokes.

America's heroes are all cut to this common mold. Whether it's George Washington, Abraham Lincoln, Davy Crockett, Thomas Edison, Henry Ford, Amelia Earhart, Jackie Robinson, Ronald Reagan, or Colin Powell, the theme is always the same: the common man against the odds. America's political romance is *Mr. Smith Goes to Washington* to make things right. It is *Meet John Doe*, who speaks for the voiceless. It is Luke Skywalker who saves the planet by using the good side of the Force to defeat the Empire. It is the odyssey of individuals who challenge power, overcome adversity, and rise to the top.

The cause of the underdog wins American hearts because it resonates with our deepest religious and moral convictions of doing good and helping others. And because it is America's own story. We began as a small nation, standing up to the world's most powerful empire. We dedicated ourselves to the idea that all men are created equal. We are a nation of immigrants and a generous people who arrived with nothing and made fortunes in a new world. This is the American dream. It is a story that will get you every time. But at election time, Democrats know how to wield it as a political weapon, and Republicans generally don't.

In deploying this weapon, Democrats use a version of the story that has a partisan edge. Through their grip on the media and the academic culture, leftists have rewritten America's past. They have transformed it from an epic of freedom into a tale of racism, exploitation, and oppression. In their version, it is no longer a story of expanding opportunity, where men and women succeed against the odds. They have turned it, instead, into a Marxist morality play about the powerful and their victims.

During the 2000 presidential election campaign, that's what the Democrats' "hate crimes" issue was really about. It was not about punishing hate crimes. It was about setting the stage for a political melodrama in which Republicans would be cast as the villains. Democrats invariably claim to speak in the name of America's "victims"—women, children, minorities, and the poor—while depicting Republicans as injuring the weak, ignoring the vulnerable, and trampling on the powerless.

And every time, Republicans walk right into the Democrats' trap because they approach politics as a management problem. To Republicans, every issue is administrative—the utility of a tax, the efficiency of a program, the optimal method for running an enterprise. Republicans talk like businessmen who want a chance to govern the country so that it will turn a profit.

There is nothing wrong with instituting good policies and running things efficiently. But while Republicans are performing these Gold Star tasks, Democrats are busy attacking Republicans as servants of the rich, oppressors of the weak, and defenders of the strong. And this is the drama that stirs emotions and brings voters to the polls.

Democrats are able to connect emotionally with people's fears and concerns because they directly engage the myth of the underdog: "I will fight for you against the powerful" is the populist mantra Al Gore used in the presidential race to good effect. Although Gore was himself part of the power elite, a *Business Week*/Harris poll taken right after the Democratic convention showed that three-quarters of the public agreed with his attacks on big oil, pharmaceutical companies, and HMOs.[23]

The appeal to help the underdog and defend the victim resonates with all Americans, not just Democrats. This is because Americans are a fair-minded people. Most successful Americans came from humble origins themselves. They want to help others. They want everyone to have the chance to succeed. So do Republicans. But Republicans rarely connect their policies and principles to this political romance.

Politics isn't just about reality. If it were, good principles and good policies would win every time. It's about images and symbols and the emotions they evoke. This is a battle that Republicans almost invariably lose.

In the romance of the victim, as Democrats stage it, Republicans are always on the side of the bad guys—the powerful, the male, the white, and the wealthy. The romance of the victim stirs the souls of the Democrats' supporters and energizes their base. But there's nothing to stop Republicans from using this romance too by turning the oppression myth around. In fact, using the romance of the underdog against the Democrats is the best way to neutralize their attack.

The most powerful forces oppressing poor and minority Americans, robbing them of opportunity, are the Democratic Party and its political creation, the welfare state. Republicans already oppose the policies of the Democrats as obstacles to the production of wealth and barriers to opportunity for all Americans. What they don't do is put a human face on the consequences of these policies; they don't connect them emotionally to the story of victims and victimizers.

The way Republicans address the problem of the welfare system is a good example of the problem. Democrats view taxes as contributions to charity. Consequently, when Democrats designed a welfare system that cost taxpayers trillions, they considered it a double good deed. Welfare taxes benefited the poor and forced Americans to do the right thing. Over the years, however, it became clear that government charity dollars were actually producing a social disaster—driving fathers from their children, bribing teenage girls to have children out of wedlock, subsidizing drug abuse, and destroying the work ethic of entire inner city communities.

To address the problem, Republicans proposed welfare reforms that would put recipients to work and get others off the rolls. Democrats said no and dug in their heels. They had to defend the vast patronage system that welfare created for government bureaucrats, social workers, and other beneficiaries who could be counted on to vote for the Democrats.

But Democrats also knew that the romance of the victim would work in their favor. When Republicans proposed welfare reform, Democrats attacked them as mean spirited and heartless. They said Republicans lacked compassion. They said Republicans were attacking the poor. They were *Nazis*.

Powerful moral images like this don't go away. They linger beyond the battle and resonate through future conflicts. In 1996, when Dick Morris persuaded Clinton to sign the Republican welfare bill "or lose the election,"[24] the images of Republicans—anti-poor and uncharitable—stuck. Clinton won the election and presided over the Republican welfare reform, claiming it as his own. It is now part of his "legacy," while Republicans are still seen as mean spirited and uncaring.

Republicans assisted in their own political undoing when they put the arguments for welfare reform in management terms. In proposing reforms, Republicans did not call welfare mothers to Washington to testify against a system that was breaking up their families, destroying their children, and blighting their communities. They did not call Democrats "racists" for not caring about the destructive impact the welfare system had on inner-city populations. They did not call them "Nazis." Instead, Republicans argued that the welfare system was "wasteful" and "inefficient," that it "wasn't working," and that it was an impediment to balancing the federal budget.

But welfare is a human problem. It isn't about economic budgets. It is about the destruction of human lives. Republicans were not oblivious to the human reality of the Democrats' welfare nightmare. They spoke about it. But they did not attempt to speak in the name of the underclass, as the champions of the underclass, or to frame a moral indictment of the Democrats that would be the focus of their campaign. They did not invoke the romance of the underdog or use the language of victimization and oppression. They did not portray the Democrats as racist oppressors and enemies of the poor.

As a result, the debate about welfare took place on the Democrats' turf. It became an argument about whether the government should spend more or less on the poor—on "charity." Republicans allowed themselves to be put in the position of arguing that government should spend less. Democrats wanted to spend more. When the debate was framed in these terms, it seemed like Democrats cared more about the poor because they were willing to spend more on them. It was easy for Democrats to portray Republicans as stingy, mean spirited, heartless, and uncaring. Republicans did it to themselves.

If the argument is about budgets, more money for welfare appears as greater generosity to the poor. But the truth is just the opposite. The Democrats' welfare programs are destructive to the poor. More money spent on welfare is more money spent on a system that is blighting the lives of millions of families.

Republicans should not have allowed the debate to be about government inefficiency and waste, about "welfare queens" rifling the public purse. They should have made it about the *harm* government does to welfare recipients. They should have made it about government programs that destroyed the lives of poor and minority people (while allowing some to benefit unjustly). If Republicans had insisted on *those* terms, Democrats would be bearing the stigma today, and Newt Gingrich and the Republican Congress would be seen as the heroes of minorities and the poor.

Instead, the welfare system was reformed and millions of poor people were freed from the chains that Democrats forged.[25] But because Republicans failed to stick Democrats with responsibility for the suffering their policies caused, Bill Clinton and Al Gore were able to claim credit for a welfare reform they resisted and that half their party opposed. Republicans lost a political issue, and Democrats were able to continue the myths they had created to defend the system, eventually undermining the reforms and then undoing them.

Another issue as important and concerning as welfare is education. Democrats are regularly billed as the "education party." How is that possible? There is a human tragedy enveloping America's inner cities. Twelve million poor children, mainly black and Hispanic, are trapped in failing government schools that are teaching them nothing. As a result, they will never get a shot at the American dream. Virtually every school board and every administration in inner city districts is controlled by Democrats and has been for over fifty years. Everything that is wrong with inner-city schools that policy can fix, Democrats are responsible for.

How bad *is* the inner-city school crisis? In Los Angeles, the school district recently defined the problem. Officials had declared their intention to end the practice of "social promotion," a scheme invented by progressives, in the name of self-esteem, to deceive students into believing that they are learning something when they are not. Instead of holding back failing students, public schools across the country promote them until they "graduate." It's only after graduation, when they enter the economy to look for a job and start a life, that they discover they are functionally illiterate and have been cheated of their opportunity to get ahead in life.

But in January 2000, the LA schools announced that they would have to postpone the cancelation of social promotion. The reason? A feasibility study showed that if the plan were instituted, officials would have to hold back 350,000 students—*half* the entire school population.[26]

Half the entire school population is learning nothing! This is an atrocity. It is no secret that these children are poor and Hispanic or black, and that for them an education is the only chance they will ever have for a better life. But Democrat-controlled schools are teaching them nothing! They will never become part of the new information economy. They will never get decent paying jobs.

It gets worse. Shortly after the school district's announcement, the Los Angeles teachers' union demanded a 21 percent pay increase for its members. The head of the union announced that his members would strike if bonuses were given as rewards to individual teachers who actually raised their students' grades. That would be setting teacher against teacher. That would be competition. Capitalism!

Where is the Republican outrage? Where are the Republican voices exposing this hypocrisy and holding the Democrats to account? Instead of issuing moral indictments of the Democrats for defending the existing system, instead of stigmatizing them as enemies of impoverished school children, Republicans do what? They approach the problem timidly and discreetly. They distance themselves from the conservative voucher movement and make legislative proposals that are modest and "reasonable." They put forward bills that are designed to win over members of the opposition.

But this ignores the reality of the system the Democrats have created, which provides billions of federal dollars to enrich adults and to secure their political loyalty at the expense of the children. Democrats will not become "reasonable" until the American people understand what they are doing. The only way this will happen is if Republicans make the Democrats' oppression of poor and minority children the focus of their political attack.

THE BATTLE AHEAD

Republicans are still mainly a rural and white party. This does not mean they are also a racist party, as Democrats maliciously suggest. It is the Democrats who are the party of racial preferences and racial politics, who have cynically exploited the loyalty of their minority supporters to the detriment of minority communities.

It has been said of the electoral map, which indicates Republican majorities in red, that every red zone marks a county in which people can still leave their doors unlocked. It is among Republicans that the virtues of the American Founding are preserved and actively defended, and it is over these principles that the culture war is being waged. But since Republicans are a rural party, they will become a minority party if they do not begin to make greater inroads into urban and ethnic America.

No party can achieve a majority in America without embracing its diverse communities. In the 2000 election, George Bush made a greater effort than any previous Republican to reach out to minority communities. Yet he was rewarded with an even smaller percentage of the African-American vote. Some Republican strategists have concluded that pursuing minority votes is a losing proposition. Instead, they advise Republicans to concentrate on increasing their majority among white Americans.

Such a strategy, born of frustration, would be a dead end for the Republican Party. It would go against the very principles of the Republican cause. Democrats are the party who believe in racial categories and "identity politics," who presume that individuals and their attitudes are determined by skin color and gender. Democrats are the party that insists that the laws and even the census should divide Americans by race, that makes the non-American end of the national hyphen the part that is important. Democrats are the party of racial caucuses, racial quotas, and racial targets.

Republicans believe in inclusion based on individual merit and individual rights. They support the principle that everyone should be judged by a single standard. They insist that the "American" end of the hyphen should be the one that counts. Republicans are—and must be—the optimists of inclusion, defenders of the proposition that opportunity should be open equally to all regardless of race, national origin, or creed. If Republicans surrender these core beliefs and accept the Balkanized future of the Left, there will be no battle for America. It will all be over. But if they don't, if they are willing to fight for what they believe, the story will have an entirely different outcome to the benefit of all.

ACKNOWLEDGMENTS

I n the writing of this volume, I am indebted to Michael B., my mentor in electoral politics, and to Craig Snider, who drew me back into the electoral fray.

I owe a special thanks to Tom Spence, my editor at Regnery and sometime head of Spence Publishing, who in that capacity published three of my books when no one else would: *Hating Whitey and Other Progressive Causes* (1999), *The Art of Political War and Other Radical Pursuits* (2000), and *How to Beat the Democrats and Other Subversive Ideas* (2002).

John Perazzo, Mike Bauer, and Sara Dogan provided invaluable assistance with the editing and research, and Elizabeth Ruiz was there with any other help I needed.

As I am constantly under attack by my political opponents, I am particularly grateful for the strength my writing has gained through the support of my colleagues, especially Michael Finch, Peter Collier, Jamie Glazov, and Ben Shapiro. I also could not have done this without the support, both moral and financial, of the board and sponsors of the David Horowitz Freedom Center.

My greatest debt is to my family. My wife, April, has made my burdens light and my days of happiness plentiful and long; my sister-in-law, Kim, has been a rock of support in a difficult health year; my children, Jon, Ben, and Anne, and my stepson, Jon Kibbie, have made their father proud with their extraordinary achievements, and also strong in their love and the love of their families. My gracious daughter-in-law, Felicia, and her family have been ever ready to fan the flames of the spirit in me when they had a tendency to ebb. And my grandchildren, Jules, Mariah, Sophie, and Elvis, have made these latter years fulfilling ones, while giving me reasons to stay in the fight.

INTRODUCTION: HAPPY WARRIORS

1. Robert Rector, senior research fellow at the Heritage Foundation, testimony before the House Budget Committee, May 3, 2012, available online at http://www.heritage.org/research/testimony/2012/05/examining-the-means-tested-welfare-state. To put this figure in perspective, Rector adds, "In comparison, the cost of all military wars in U.S. history from the Revolutionary War through the current war in Afghanistan has been $6.98 trillion (in inflation-adjusted 2011 dollars). The War on Poverty has cost three times as much as all other wars combined."

2. "How Many Trillions Must We Waste on the War on Poverty?," Conn Carroll, *Foundry* (blog), Heritage Foundation, March 17, 2011, http://blog.heritage.org/2011/03/17/morning-bell-how-many-trillions-must-we-waste-on-the-war-on-poverty/.

3. Restoration Weekend was originally called "The Dark Ages Weekend" and was created by Laura Ingraham and Jay Lefkowitz, who passed it on to me in 1996. The original name was inspired by the Clintons' event and was intended as a bit of black humor satirizing the Democrats' malicious view of conservatives as anti-Enlightenment reactionaries bent on turning back the historical clock. However, Republicans like House Speaker Newt Gingrich felt the joke would backfire and boycotted the event, which was why, when I inherited it, I changed the name.

4.   Obama advisor Cass Sunstein has even co-authored a soft version of this coercive
      vision called *Nudge: Improving Decisions about Health, Wealth, and Happiness*
      (New Haven: Yale University Press, 2009).

5.   "Obamacare: Before And After," DiscoverTheNetworks.org, http://www.
      discoverthenetworks.org/viewSubCategory.asp?id=1957.

CHAPTER 1: GO FOR THE HEART

1.   Jeff Poor, "Obama Has No Choice but 'to Go Negative and Go Negative Hard,'"
      Daily Caller, June 5, 2012.

2.   Beth Reinhard, "The Numbers behind Obama's Negative Ad Campaign,"
      National Journal, July 12, 2012, http://www.nationaljournal.com/2012-
      presidential-campaign/the-numbers-behind-obama-s-negative-ad-
      campaign-20120712.

3.   Heather Higgins and Alex Cortes, "The Phrase That Lost Romney the Election,"
      Real Clear Politics, November 23, 2012, http://www.realclearpolitics.com/articles
      /2012/11/23/the_phrase_that_lost_romney_the_election_116235.html.

4.   Dick Morris, *Behind the Oval Office: Winning the Presidency in the Nineties* (New
      York: Random House, 1997), 268.

5.   It was, of course, Obama's chief of staff Rahm Emanuel who said, "You never
      want a serious crisis to go to waste. And what I mean by that [is] it's an oppor-
      tunity to do things you think you could not do before." "Rahm Emanuel: You
      Never Want a Serious Crisis to Go to Waste," YouTube video, from speech to *Wall
      Street Journal* CEO Council, posted by "Jim Swift," February 9, 2009, http://www.
      youtube.com/watch?v=1yeA_kHHLow. On the other hand, to his credit, when
      Emanuel saw the magnitude of the opposition to Obamacare, he opposed pur-
      suing the legislation.

6.   Molly Moorhead, "Sandra Fluke on Contraceptives and Women's Health," *Politi-
      Fact*, March 6, 2012, http://www.politifact.com/truth-o-meter/article/2012/
      mar/06/context-sandra-fluke-contraceptives-and-womens-hea/.

7.   See, for example, news commentator Barbara Walters: "We thought that he was
      going to be—I shouldn't say this at Christmastime, but—the next messiah."
      Melanie Batley, "Barbara Walters: We Thought Obama Was 'the Next Messiah,'"
      Newsmax, December 18, 2013, http://www.newsmax.com/Newsfront/Barbara-
      Walters-obama-next-messiah/2013/12/18/id/542573#ixzz2pw86mYed.

8.   "Transcript: Illinois Senate Candidate Barack Obama," transcript of Barack
      Obama's keynote address at the 2004 Democratic National Convention in

Boston, available online at *Washington Post*, July 27, 2004, http://www. washingtonp ost.com/wp-dyn/articles/A19751-2004Jul27.html.

9. "Obama Takes On GOP's Economic 'Prescription' at DNC," *Fox News Insider* (blog), Fox News, September 6, 2012, http://foxnewsinsider.com/2012/09/06/ obama-takes-on-gops-economic-prescription-at-dnc-take-two-tax-cuts-roll-back-some-regulations-and-call-us-in-the-morning.

10. Patricia Zengerle, "Democrats Charge Republicans with 'War on Women' at Convention," Reuters, September 4, 2012, http://www.reuters.com/ article/2012/09/05/us-usa-campaign-women-idUSBRE88401T20120905.

11. "Mario Cuomo Speaks at the Democratic National Convention," transcript of speech given at 1996 Democratic National Convention, available online at PBS NewsHour, August 27, 1996, http://www.pbs.org/newshour/bb/politics/july-dec96/cuomo_08-27.html.

12. James Hohmann, "Obama, Romney Campaign Officials Dissect 2012 Election at Dole Institute," Politico, December 8, 2012, http://www.politico.com/ story/2012/12/campaign-officials-dissect-election-cycle-84796.html.

13. "Mitt Romney's favorability ratings were on the upswing ever since he locked down the Republican nomination in April, but there are growing signs that a torrent of negative attacks from President Obama and his Democratic allies have affected voter impressions of the GOP hopeful." Christina Bellantoni and Terence Burlij, "As Negative Attacks Pile Up, Romney's Favorability Ratings Go Down," *Rundown* (blog), PBS NewsHour, August 10, 2012, http://www.pbs.org/ newshour/rundown/2012/08/romneys-favorability-declines-as-negative-attacks-pile-up.html.

14. Hohmann, "Obama, Romney Campaign Officials Dissect 2012 Election at Dole Institute."

15. Mary Bruce, "Obama Mocks Romney for Seamus the Dog," ABC News, August 14, 2012, http://abcnews.go.com/blogs/politics/2012/08/obama-mocks-romney-for-seamus-the-dog/.

16. "Obama Campaign Launches Attack on Romney's Jobs Record at Bain," Fox News, May 14, 2012, http://www.foxnews.com/politics/2012/05/14/new-obama-ad-seeks-to-undercut-romney-record-on-jobs/.

17. For the official unemployment rate of Detroit, see "Detroit, MI Unemployment Rate," http://ycharts.com/indicators/detroit_mi_unemployment_rate; and "Detroit, Michigan," http://www.city-data.com/city/Detroit-Michigan.html. The 45 percent figure was reached in 2009 and includes part-time workers who wanted full-time work and those who had given up looking for work—which the official unemployment rate doesn't include. Jonathon Oosting, "Report:

Nearly 50 Percent of Detroit's Working-Age Population Is Unemployed," MLive, December 16, 2009, http://www.mlive.com/news/detroit/index.ssf/2009/12/report_nearly_50_percent_of_de.html

18. Terence P. Jeffrey, "Obama's America Will Become Detroit," CNS News, December 12, 2012, http://cnsnews.com/blog/terence-p-jeffrey/obamas-america-will-become-detroit.

19. Rakesh Kochhar, Richard Fry, and Paul Taylor, "Wealth Gaps Rise to Record Highs between Whites, Blacks, Hispanics: Twenty-to-One," Social and Demographic Trends, Pew Research, July 26, 2011, http://www.pewsocialtrends.org/2011/07/26/wealth-gaps-rise-to-record-highs-between-whites-blacks-hispanics/.

20. See chapter 6, "Destructive Social Justice," in Part I of this volume.

21. Noel Sheppard, "Carter More to Blame for Financial Crisis Than Bush or McCain," NewsBusters, September 20, 2008, http://newsbusters.org/blogs/noel-sheppard/2008/09/20/ibd-carter-more-blame-financial-crisis-bush-or-mccain.

22. Associated Press, "Chicago Teachers Strike for First Time in 25 Years After Contract Talks Fail," Fox News, September 10, 2012, http://www.foxnews.com/us/2012/09/10/chicago-teachers-to-go-on-strike-after-talks-with-district-fail/.

CHAPTER 2: DEFEND OUR COUNTRY

1. "List of Islamic Terrorist Attacks for the Past 30 Days," TheReligionofPeace.com, accessed May 2014, http://www.thereligionofpeace.com/index.html#Attacks.

2. Jessica Yellin, "Obama Adds 'al Qaeda' Back to Stump Speech," *Political Ticker* (blog), CNN, October 18, 2012, http://politicalticker.blogs.cnn.com/2012/10/18/white-house-view-on-al-qaeda-unchanged/.

3. Scott Wilson and Al Kamen, "'Global War on Terror' Is Given New Name," *Washington Post*, March 25, 2009, http://www.washingtonpost.com/wp-dyn/content/article/2009/03/24/AR2009032402818.html.

4. Cheryl K. Chumley, "Nidal Hasan's Fort Hood Trial Starts: 'Workplace Violence' Classification Denies Purple Hearts," *Washington Times*, August 6, 2013, http://www.washingtontimes.com/news/2013/aug/6/nidal-hasans-fort-hood-trial-starts-workplace-viol/.

5. "Wong is a 2007 Harvard Law School graduate and a former associate at the law firm of Covington & Burling, but his credentials as a foreign-policy expert are thin at best, amounting to a summer internship at the U.S. mission to the U.N. in 2005 and service as a 'rule of law' adviser on Iraq at the State Department from

2007 to 2009." Michael Hirsh, "Foreign Policy: Who Has Romney's Ear?," *National Journal*, August 27, 2012, http://www.nationaljournal.com/2012-election/foreign-policy-who-has-romney-s-ear—20120827. For an insider's account of the Romney foreign policy fiasco, see Gabriel Schoenfeld, *A Bad Day on the Romney Campaign* (New York: Penguin, 2013).

6.   "Obama's Speech to the United Nations General Assembly—Text," *New York Times*, September 25, 2012, http://www.nytimes.com/2012/09/26/world/obamas-speech-to-the-united-nations-general-assembly-text.html?pagewanted=2&_r=0.

7.   For an insightful account of these developments, see Andrew C. McCarthy, *Spring Fever: The Illusion of Islamic Democracy* (New York: Encounter, 2013).

8.   Gadi Adelman, "The Cornerstone of Regional Stability and Peace," *Family Security Matters*, November 27, 2012, http://www.familysecuritymatters.org/publications/detail/the-cornerstone-of-regional-stability-and-peace.

9.   Robert Spencer, "The World's Most Popular Muslim Preacher, Yusuf al-Qaradawi, Asks Allah to Destroy the Jews," Jihad Watch, November 18, 2012, http://www.jihadwatch.org/2012/11/the-worlds-most-popular-muslim-preacher-yusuf-al-qaradawi-asks-allah-to-destroy-the-jews.html.

10.   Bridget Johnson, "Kerry: Don't 'Prejudge' the Muslim Brotherhood," PJ Media, June 24, 2012, http://pjmedia.com/tatler/2012/06/24/kerry-dont-prejudge-the-muslim-brotherhood/.

11.   Daniel Halper, "Kerry a Frequent Visitor with Syrian Dictator Bashar Al-Assad," *Weekly Standard*, December 21, 2012, http://www.weeklystandard.com/blogs/kerry-frequent-visitor-syrian-dictator-bashar-al-assad_690885.html.

12.   "Full Text of Romney's Speech," transcript of Mitt Romney's acceptance speech at the 2012 Republican National Convention, *Washington Wire* (blog), *Wall Street Journal*, August 30, 2012, http://blogs.wsj.com/washwire/2012/08/30/full-text-of-romneys-speech/.

13.   "Carter's Pollster, Patrick Caddell, believed that Iran's rebuff of [Carter's overtures] doomed Carter, saying 'It was all related to the hostages and events overseas.'" John Sides, "What Really Happened in the 1980 Presidential Campaign," *Monkey Cage* (blog), August 9, 2012, http://themonkeycage.org/2012/08/09/what-really-happened-in-the-1980-presidential-campaign/.

14.   Robert Spencer, "Huma Abedin and the Muslim Brotherhood: Bachmann vs. McCain," *FrontPage Magazine*, July 19, 2012, http://frontpagemag.com/2012/robert-spencer/huma-abedin-and-the-muslim-brotherhood-bachmann-vs-mccain/.

15.   Daniel Greenfield, "Conspiracy of Brothers," *FrontPage Magazine*, January 7, 2013, http://frontpagemag.com/2013/dgreenfield/conspiracy-of-brothers/; Frank Gaffney, *The Muslim Brotherhood in the Obama Administration* (Sherman Oaks, CA: David Horowitz Freedom Center, 2012), http://www.frontpagemag.com/upload/pamphlets/mb-in-wh.pdf.

16.   Seung Min Kim, "Boehner: Huma Abedin Allegations 'Pretty Dangerous,'" Politico, July 19, 2012, http://www.politico.com/blogs/on-congress/2012/07/boehner-huma-abedin-allegations-pretty-dangerous-129467.html.

17.   Associated Press, "Gore: Bush 'Betrayed' U.S.," Fox News, February 9, 2004, http://www.foxnews.com/story/0,2933,110830,00.html; Charles Krauthammer, "Ted Kennedy's Iraq Ravings," *FrontPage Magazine*, September 26, 2003, http://archive.frontpagemag.com/readArticle.aspx?ARTID=16183; and Larry Elder, "Bush Lied, People Died?," *Townhall*, March 2, 2006, http://townhall.com/columnists/larryelder/2006/03/02/bush_lied,_people_died/page/full/.

18.   "Transcript of the Third Presidential Debate," *New York Times*, October 22, 2012, http://www.nytimes.com/2012/10/22/us/politics/transcript-of-the-third-presidential-debate-in-boca-raton-fla.html?pagewanted=3&_r=0.

19.   This history is recounted in David Horowitz, *Unholy Alliance: Radical Islam and the American Left* (Washington, D.C.: Regnery Publishing Inc., 2004).

20.   President William J. Clinton, "Statement on Signing the Iraq Liberation Act of 1998," The American Presidency Project, University California, Santa Barbara, October 31, 1998, http://www.presidency.ucsb.edu/ws/?pid=55205.

21.   See David Horowitz and Ben Johnson, *Party of Defeat: How Democrats and Radicals Undermined America's Security before and after 9/11* (Dallas: Spence Publishing, 2008); Douglas Feith, *War and Decision: Inside the Pentagon at the Dawn of the War on Terrorism* (New York: Harper, 2008).

22.   David M. Halbfinger and David E. Sanger, "Bush and Kerry Clash over Iraq and a Timetable," *New York Times*, September 7, 2004, http://www.nytimes.com/2004/09/07/politics/campaign/07campaign.html.

23.   Michael Dobbs, "McCain's '100-Year War,'" *Washington Post*, April 2, 2008, http://voices.washingtonpost.com/fact-checker/2008/04/mccains_100year_war.html.

CHAPTER 3: THE PROGRESSIVE THREAT

1.   David Horowitz, *Radical Son: A Generational Odyssey* (New York: Free Press, 1997).

2. David Horowitz and Jacob Laksin, *One-Party Classroom* (New York: Crown Forum, 2009); David Horowitz, *Indoctrination U.* (New York: Encounter, 2007).

3. Stanley Kurtz, *Radical-In-Chief* (New York: Threshold, 2010); Paul Kengor, *The Communist: Frank Marshall Davis; The Untold Story of Barack Obama's Mentor* (New York: Mercury Ink, 2012); "Valerie Jarrett," DiscovertheNetworks.org, http://www.discoverthenetworks.org/individualProfile.asp?indid=2418; and "David Axelrod," DiscovertheNetworks.org, http://www.discoverthenetworks.org/individualProfile.asp?indid=2466.

4. "Reid: 'We Support the Federal Government. That's Our Job. That's What We Do.,'" Daniel Halper, *Weekly Standard*, October 1, 2013, http://www.weeklysta ndard.com/blogs/reid-we-support-federal-government-thats-our-job-that s-what-we-do_759044.html.

5. In fact, this radical departure goes back to the Roosevelt administration. See Gordon Lloyd and David Davenport, *The New Deal and Modern American Conservatism: A Defining Rivalry* (Stanford, CA: Hoover Institution, 2013), chapter 4.

6. See pages 2 and 7 of Itamar Marcus and Nan Jacques Zilberdik, "The Muslim Brotherhood—in Its Own Words: PMW Translation of *Jihad Is the Way* by Mustafa Mashhur," Palestinian Media Watch, http://palwatch.org/STORAGE/special%20reports/Jihad_is_the_way_by_Mustafa_Mashhur.pdf.

7. "US Supreme Court Justice Ruth Bader Ginsburg to Egyptians: Look to the Constitutions of South Africa or Canada, Not to the US Constitution," speech aired on Al-Hayat TV, January 30, 2012, Middle East Research Institute, January 30, 2012, http://www.memritv.org/clip_transcript/en/3295.htm.

8. Madison's term was "parchment rights."

9. Diana Schaub, "South Africa's Orwellian Constitution," Hoover Institution, April 4, 2012, http://www.hoover.org/publications/defining-ideas/article/113041; and "Quarter of Men in South Africa Admit Rape, Survey Finds," *Guardian*, June 17, 2009, http://www.theguardian.com/world/2009/jun/17/south-africa-rape-su rvey.

10. Schaub, "South Africa's Orwellian Constitution."

11. Roosevelt himself actually proposed a "Second Bill of Rights," based on the totalitarian model, which has been recently promoted by Cass Sunstein, one of President Obama's chief legal advisors. Cass Sunstein, *The Second Bill of Rights: FDR's Unfinished Revolution—and Why We Need It More Than Ever* (New York: Basic, 2009).

12. "The Social Contract," Jean-Jacques Rousseau (1712–1788), http://www.rjgeib.com/thoughts/rousseau/rousseau.html.

13. For a discussion of this, see Andrzej Walicki, *Marxism and the Leap to the Kingdom of Freedom: The Rise and Fall of the Communist Utopia* (Stanford: Stanford University Press, 1995).

14. Obama was trained as a "community organizer" in Alinsky schools and became an instructor in Alinsky's methods himself. See Horowitz, *Barack Obama's Rules for Revolution* (David Horowitz Freedom Center, 2009).

15. Saul Alinsky, *Rules for Radicals* (New York: Random House, 1971), 24.

16. Horowitz, *Barack Obama's Rules For Revolution*. A revised version of this essay is included as a chapter in David Horowitz, *Radicals: Portraits of a Destructive Passion* (Washington, D.C.: Regnery, 2012).

17. "Obamacare: Before And After," DiscovertheNetworks.org, http://www.disc overthenetworks.org/viewSubCategory.asp?id=1957.

18. Drew Gonshorowski, "How Will You Fare in the Obamacare Exchanges?" Heritage Foundation, October 16, 2013, http://www.heritage.org/research/ reports/2013/10/enrollment-in-obamacare-exchanges-how-will-your-health-insurance-fare; and "49-State Analysis: Obamacare to Increase Individual-Market Premiums by Average of 41%," Avik Roy, *Forbes*, November 4, 2013, http://www.forbes.com/sites/theapothecary/2013/11/04/49-state-analysis-oba macare-to-increase-individual-market-premiums-by-avg-of-41-subsidies-flow-to-elderly/.

19. "The Scheme behind the Obamacare Fraud," Andrew C. McCarthy, *National Review*, November 23, 2013, http://www.nationalreview.com/article/364667/ scheme-behind-obamacare-fraud-andrew-c-mccarthy.

20. On this aspect of progressivism, see Horowitz, *The Black Book of the American Left* ,vol. 2, *Progressives* (David Horowitz Freedom Center, 2014).

21. Martha Nussbaum and Joshua Cohen, *For Love of Country?* (Boston: Beacon Press, 2002).

22. "Benghazi: The Terrorist Attack of September 11, 2012," DiscovertheNetworks. org, http://www.discoverthenetworks.org/viewSubCategory.asp?id=1755.

23. Nicholas Ballasy, "Panetta Can't Explain Why Obama Never Called Back during Benghazi Attack," Daily Caller, February 7, 2013, http://dailycaller. com/2013/02/07/panetta-cant-explain-why-obama-never-called-back-during-benghazi-attack-video/#.

24. Daniel Halper, "Clinton Shouts: 'What Difference … Does It Make?,'" *Weekly Standard*, January 23, 2013, http://www.weeklystandard.com/blogs/clinton-shouts-what-difference-would-it-make_697536.html.

25.   William J. Clinton, "Statement on Signing the Iraq Liberation Act of 1998," available online at the *American Presidency Project*, University of California, Santa Barbara, October 31, 1998, http://www.presidency.ucsb.edu/ws/?pid=55205.

26.   "Security Council Holds Iraq in 'Material Breach' of Disarmament Obligations, Offers Final Chance to Comply, Unanimous Adopting Resolution 1441 (2002)," press release, United Nations Security Council, August 11, 2002, http://www.un.org/News/Press/docs/2002/SC7564.doc.htm; and Horowitz, *Unholy Alliance: Radical Islam and the American Left* (Washington, D.C.: Regnery Publishing, 2004), 26, 218.

27.   Daniel Greenfield, *The Great Betrayal: Obama's Wars and the War in Iraq* (David Horowitz Freedom Center, 2012). Kindle edition.

CHAPTER 4: FIGHT FIRE WITH FIRE

1.   These developments are explained, analyzed, and documented in David Horowitz and Jacob Laksin, *The New Leviathan: How the Left-Wing Money-Machine Shapes American Politics and Threatens America's Future* (New York: Crown Forum, 2012).

2.   "George Soros," DiscovertheNetworks.org, http://www.discoverthenetworks.org/individualProfile.asp?indid=977.

3.   "Obama Campaign Launches Attack on Romney's Jobs Record at Bain," Fox News, May 14, 2012, http://www.foxnews.com/politics/2012/05/14/new-obama-ad-seeks-to-undercut-romney-record-on-jobs/.

4.   "The Affordable Care Act is the most powerful law for reducing health disparities since Medicare and Medicaid were created in 1965, the same year the Voting Rights Act was also enacted.... The same arguments against change, the same fear and misinformation that opponents used then are the same ones opponents are spreading now." Rick Moran, "Sebelius Tells NAACP Obamacare Opponents like White Racists Who Opposed Civil Rights," *American Thinker* (blog), July 18, 2013, http://www.americanthinker.com/blog/2013/07/sebelius_tells_naacp_obamacare_opponents_like_white_racists_who_opposed_civil_rights.html.

5.   Andrew Kirell, "Tavis Smiley: Black People Are Not Better Off under Obama; President Ought to Be 'Held Responsible,'" Mediaite, October 12, 2013, http://www.mediaite.com/tv/tavis-smiley-black-people-are-not-better-off-under-obama-president-ought-to-be-held-responsible/.

6.   Kevin D. Williamson, *What Doomed Detroit* (New York: Encounter, 2013).

7.   Arnold Ahlert, "How the Democrats Destroyed Detroit," *FrontPage Magazine*, March 4, 2013, http://www.frontpagemag.com/2013/arnold-ahlert/how-the-democrats-destroyed-detroit/.

8.   Ibid.

9.   Robert Rector, "Marriage: America's Greatest Weapon against Child Poverty," Heritage Foundation, September 5, 2012, http://www.heritage.org/research/reports/2012/09/marriage-americas-greatest-weapon-against-child-poverty.

10. The city's adults have an illiteracy rate of 47 percent, and half of those who are illiterate have high school diplomas. "Nearly Half of Detroiters Can't Read," CBS Detroit, May 4, 2011, http://detroit.cbslocal.com/2011/05/04/report-nearly-half-of-detroiters-cant-read/; and "Addressing Detroit's Basic Skills Crisis," Detroit Regional Workforce Fund, May 2011, http://cbsdetroit.files.wordpress.com/2011/05/basicskillsreport_final.pdf.

11. "Philanthropist Withdraws $200 Million for Detroit Charter Schools," Philanthropy News Digest, October 8, 2003, http://www.philanthropynewsdigest.org/news/philanthropist-withdraws-200-million-for-detroit-charter-schools.

12. Class size according to the National Center for Education Statistics, "Teachers, Enrollment, and Pupil/Teacher Ratios in Public Elementary and Secondary Schools, by State or Jurisdiction: Selected Years, Fall 2000 through Fall 2007," Digest of Education Statistics, http://nces.ed.gov/programs/digest/d09/tables/dt09_066.asp.

13. Andrew J. Coulson, "Census Bureau Confirms: DC Spends $29,409/Pupil," Cato Institute, June 26, 2012, http://www.cato.org/blog/census-bureau-confirms-dc-spends-29409-pupil; and Michael McShane, "D.C. Public Schools Grossly Under-Reports Spending," Huffington Post, June 29, 2012, http://www.huffingtonpost.com/michael-mcshane/dc-public-schools-grossly_b_1638663.html.

14. Adrian Fenty and Michelle Rhee, "The Education Manifesto," *Wall Street Journal*, October 30, 2010, http://online.wsj.com/news/articles/SB10001424052702303362404575580221511231074.

15. For an analysis of this movement, see David Horowitz and John Perazzo, *Occupy Wall Street: The Communist Movement Reborn* (David Horowitz Freedom Center, 2012). Ebook edition.

CHAPTER 5: UNITING THE RIGHT

1.   "Obama: Fundamentally Transforming the United States of America," YouTube video, from speech given by Barack Obama at the University of Missouri in

Columbia, Missouri, October 30, 2008, uploaded by "jbranstetter04," May 20, 2011, http://www.youtube.com/watch?v=KrefKCaV8m4.

2.   Speech at the Thirteenth Congress of the Russian Communist Party, held in Moscow, May 23–31, 1924.

3.   Saul Alinsky, *Rules for Radicals* (New York: Random House, 1971), 134.

4.   "'As frustrating as HealthCare.gov may be sometimes,' Obama told ObamaCare navigators and volunteers, 'We're on the right side of history.'" Daniel Greenfield, "The Left Side of History," *FrontPage Magazine*, November 18, 2013, http://www. frontpagemag.com/2013/dgreenfield/the-left-side-of-history/.

5.   Jonathan Turley, "Lies like a Rug: New Obama Rug Has Historical Quote Wrong," *Jonathan Turley* (blog), September 6, 2010, http://jonathanturley.org/2010/09/06/ lies-like-a-rug-new-obama-rug-has-historical-quote-wrong/; and Jamie Stiehm, "Oval Office Rug Gets History Wrong," *Washington Post*, September 4, 2010, http://www.washingtonpost.com/wp-dyn/content/article/2010/09/03/ AR2010090305100.html.

6.   The Federalist No. 10.

7.   Ibid.

CHAPTER 6: DESTRUCTIVE SOCIAL JUSTICE

1.   "'The Era of Big Government Is Over,'" transcript of President Clinton's radio address, available online at CNN, January 27, 1996, http://www.cnn.com/ US/9601/budget/01-27/clinton_radio/.

2.   Bill Clinton, *Back to Work: Why We Need Smart Government for a Strong Economy* (New York: Knopf, 2011).

3.   Stephen Moore, "Like the '90s Never Happened," *Wall Street Journal*, November 8, 2011, http://online.wsj.com/article/SB1000142405297020419070457702416 0426640058.html.

4.   "Occupy Wall Street," Discover the Networks, http://www.discoverthenetworks. org/groupProfile.asp?grpid=7694.

5.   Clinton, *Back to Work*.

6.   George Will, "Mugged by Data: Research Reveals Who the Truly Compassionate Are," *Jewish World Review*, March 27, 2008, http://jewishworldreview.com/cols/ will032708.php3.

7.   Rakesh Kochhar, Richard Fry, and Paul Taylor, "Wealth Gaps Rise to Record Highs between Whites, Blacks, Hispanics," Pew Research, Social & Demographic

Trends, July 26, 2011, http://www.pewsocialtrends.org/2011/07/26/wealth-gaps-rise-to-record-highs-between-whites-blacks-hispanics/.

8. Economic Policy Institute, "Homeownership Rate, by Race and Ethnicity, 1975–2011," The State of Working America, updated August 24, 2012, http://stateofworkingamerica.org/chart/swa-wealth-figure-6j-homeownership-rate/.

9. Adam Clymer, "Henry Reuss, Liberal in Congress, Dies at 89," *New York Times*, January 15, 2002, http://www.nytimes.com/2002/01/15/us/henry-reuss-liberal-in-congress-dies-at-89.html.

10. Electronic Code of Federal Regulations, Title 12, Part 25, "Community Reinvestment Act and Interstate Deposit Production Regulations," available online at http://www.ecfr.gov/cgi-bin/text-idx?c=ecfr&sid=52a4960633093ddafec27270 93859f12&rgn=div5&view=text&node=12:1.0.1.1.23&idno=12.

11. Courtesy of the Public Services Division, Law Library of Congress.

12. Thomas Sowell, *The Housing Boom and Bust* (New York: Basic Books, 2009) 36–37.

13. Howard Husock, "The Trillion-Dollar Bank Shakedown That Bodes Ill for Cities," *City Journal*, Winter 2000, http://www.city-journal.org/html/10_1_the_trillion _dollar.html.

14. Sol Stern, "ACORN's Nutty Regime for Cities," *City Journal*, Spring 2003, http://www.city-journal.org/html/13_2_acorns_nutty_regime.html; Husock, "The Trillion-Dollar Bank Shakedown That Bodes Ill for Cities"; and Stanley Kurtz, *Radical-in-Chief: Barack Obama and the Untold Story of American Socialism* (New York: Threshold Editions, 2010).

15. Sowell, *The Vision of the Anointed* (New York: Basic Books, 1995), 41.

16. Sowell, *The Housing Boom and Bust*, 108.

17. Sowell, *The Vision of the Anointed*.

18. Ibid.

19. Raphael W. Bostic, "The Role of Race in Mortgage Lending: Revisiting the Boston Fed Study," working paper, Division of Research and Statistics—Federal Reserve Board of Governors, December 1996, http://www.federalreserve.gov/pubs/feds/1997/199702/199702pap.pdf.

20. Sowell, *The Vision of the Anointed*, 104.

21. Larry Elder, "Blacks, Banks and 'Institutional Racism,'" Creators Syndicate, July 19, 2007, http://www.creators.com/opinion/larry-elder/blacks-banks-and-institutional-racism.html.

22. Ibid.

23. Luke Ford, "Which Racial Groups Are the Most Likely to Default on Loans?," Mortgage Refinance News & Tips, March 30, 2011, http://www.refinancemortga

genow.net/2011/03/; and Richard Anderson and James VanderHoff, "Mortgage Default Rates and Borrower Race," Journal Of Real Estate Research 18, no. 2 (1999), http://aux.zicklin.baruch.cuny.edu/jrer/papers/pdf/past/vol18n02/v18p279.pdf.

24. The foregoing findings were amplified in subsequent research. In 1998, it was reported that the data used by the original Boston Fed study contained hundreds of errors vis-à-vis such variables as the net worth of the applicants and the interest rates of the loans they sought. When those data errors were corrected, evidence suggesting that lenders had discriminated against minority borrowers disappeared. In 1999, the *Journal of Real Estate Research* (vol. 18, no. 2) reported that black households had "higher marginal default rates" and "lower equity" than white households; the authors could find no evidence "consistent with racial discrimination in mortgage lending."

25. Vern McKinley, "Community Reinvestment Act: Ensuring Credit Adequacy or Enforcing Credit Allocation?," Cato Institute, October 11, 1994, http://www.cato.org/regulation/fall-1994/community-reinvestment-act; and "Policy Statement on Discrimination in Lending," Department of Housing and Urban Development 59, no. 73 (April 15, 1994), http://www.gpo.gov/fdsys/pkg/FR-1994-04-15/html/94-9214.htm. Subprime mortgages were loans characterized by higher interest rates and less favorable terms designed to compensate lenders for the high credit risk they were incurring.

26. Carl Horowitz, "Affirmative Action for Banks?," *Investor's Business Daily*, March 31, 1995, http://news.investors.com/033195-327257-affirmative-action-for-banks-.htm.

27. Husock, "The Trillion-Dollar Bank Shakedown That Bodes Ill for Cities."

28. "Community Reinvestment Act—Ratings," *FDIC Compliance Manual* 11, June 2006, http://www.fdic.gov/regulations/compliance/manual/pdf/XI-6.1.pdf.

29. McKinley, "Community Reinvestment Act."

30. Matthew Vadum, *Subversion, Inc.: How Obama's ACORN Red Shirts Are Still Terrorizing and Ripping Off American Taxpayers* (Washington, D.C.: WND Books, 2011).

31. "The Role of the Community Reinvestment Act in the Financial Crisis," Cato Institute, November 18, 2009, http://www.cato.org/events/role-community-reinvestment-act-financial-crisis.

32. McKinley, "Community Reinvestment Act."

33. Lawrence H. White, "How Did We Get into This Financial Mess?," Cato Institute Briefing Paper, no. 110, November 18, 2008, http://www.cato.org/pubs/bp/bp110.pdf.

34.   Ibid.

35.   Ibid.

36.   Ron Nixon, "Study Predicts Foreclosure for 1 in 5 Subprime Loans," *New York Times*, December 20, 2006, http://www.nytimes.com/2006/12/20/business/20home.html?_r=1.

37.   Sowell, "Is Barney Frank?," Creators Syndicate, October 19, 2010, http://www.creators.com/opinion/thomas-sowell/is-barney-frank.html.

38.   Editors, "Don't Bank on This Bill," editorial, *National Review*, June 26, 2010, http://www.nationalreview.com/articles/243350/dont-bank-bill-editors.

39.   "The American Dream Downpayment Initiative," U.S. Department of Housing and Urban Development, http://portal.hud.gov/hudportal/HUD?src=/program_offices/comm_planning/affordablehousing/programs/home/addi.

40.   "Bush Administration Announces New HUD 'Zero Down Payment' Mortgage," news release no. 04-006, U.S. Department of Housing and Urban Development, January 19, 2004, http://archives.hud.gov/news/2004/pr04-006.cfm.

41.   Sowell, *The Housing Boom and Bust*, 42.

42.   Ibid.

43.   Debbie Gruenstein Bocian, Wei Li, and Keith S. Ernst, "Foreclosures by Race and Ethnicity: The Demographics of a Crisis," Center For Responsible Lending, June 18, 2010, http://www.responsiblelending.org/mortgage-lending/research-analysis/foreclosures-by-race-and-ethnicity.pdf.

44.   Annie Lowrey, "Race and the Foreclosure Crisis," *Washington Independent*, June 18, 2010, http://washingtonindependent.com/87440/race-and-the-foreclosure-crisis.

45.   Gruenstein Bocian, Li, and Ernst, "Foreclosures by Race and Ethnicity."

46.   Board of Governors of the Federal Reserve System, "Report to the Congress on Credit Scoring and Its Effects on the Availability and Affordability of Credit," August 2007, p. O-13, http://www.federalreserve.gov/boarddocs/rptcongress/creditscore/creditscore.pdf.

47.   Sowell, *The Housing Boom and Bust*, 101.

48.   Andrew Jakabovics and Jeff Chapman, "Unequal Opportunity Lenders? Analyzing Racial Disparities in Big Banks' Higher-Priced Lending," Center For American Progress, September 2009, http://www.americanprogress.org/issues/2009/09/pdf/tarp_report.pdf.

49.   "State of Hispanic Ownership Report," National Association of Hispanic Real Estate Professionals, 2012, http://nahrep.org/downloads/state-of-homeownership.pdf.

50.   Sowell, *The Housing Boom and Bust*, 107–8.

51. *State of Hispanic Ownership Report, National Association of Hispanic Real Estate Professionals*, 2012, http://nahrep.org/downloads/state-of-homeownership.pdf; and Kai Wright, "The Assault on the Black Middle Class," *American Prospect*, June 26, 2009, http://prospect.org/article/assault-black-middle-class.

52. Kochhar, Fry, and Taylor, "Wealth Gaps Rise to Record Highs between Whites, Blacks, Hispanics."

53. Ibid.

54. Ben Rooney, "Recession Worsens Racial Wealth Gap," CNN Money, July 26, 2011, http://money.cnn.com/2011/07/26/news/economy/wealth_gap_white_black_hispanic/index.htm.

55. Russell Contreras, "Urban League: Black Middle Class Losing Ground," CNS News, July 27, 2011, http://cnsnews.com/news/article/urban-league-black-middle-class-losing-ground.

56. Byron York, "Dems Push Expanded Community Reinvestment Act; Dismiss Evidence That CRA Contributed to Financial Meltdown; Republicans Cite ACORN Connection," *Washington Examiner*, September 16, 2009, http://royce.house.gov/news/documentsingle.aspx?DocumentID=145193.

57. U.S. Department of the Treasury, *Income Mobility in the U.S. from 1996 to 2005*, November 13, 2007, revised March 2008, http://www.treasury.gov/resource-center/tax-policy/Documents/incomemobilitystudy03-08revise.pdf; and Thomas A. Garrett, "U.S. Income Inequality: It's Not So Bad," Federal Reserve Bank of St. Louis, Spring 2010, http://www.stlouisfed.org/publications/itv/articles/?id=1920.

58. Ibid.

59. Michael Eric Dyson, "Obama's Rebuke of Absentee Black Fathers," *Time*, June 19, 2008, http://www.time.com/time/magazine/article/0,9171,1816485,00.html.

60. Robert Rector, "Married Fathers: America's Greatest Weapon against Child Poverty," Heritage Foundation, June 16, 2010, http://www.heritage.org/research/reports/2010/06/married-fathers-americas-greatest-weapon-against-child-poverty.

61. Marjorie Hunter, "Johnson Signs Bill to Fight Poverty; Pledges New Era," *New York Times*, August 21, 1964, p. 1.

62. Sowell, *The Vision of the Anointed*, 11.

63. President Lyndon B. Johnson, "Commencement Address at Howard University: 'To Fulfill These Rights,'" transcript of speech given on June 4, 1965, available online at http://www.lbjlib.utexas.edu/johnson/archives.hom/speeches.hom/650604.asp.

64. Peter Ferrara, "America's Ever Expanding Welfare Empire," *Forbes*, April 22, 2011, http://www.forbes.com/sites/peterferrara/2011/04/22/americas-ever-expanding-welfare-empire/print/.

65. Don Lee and Alana Semuels, "1 in 7 in U.S. Lives Below Poverty Line," *Los Angeles Times*, September 17, 2010, http://articles.latimes.com/2010/sep/17/business/la-fi-poverty-census-20100917; and "Current Population Survey," U.S. Census Bureau, U.S. Department of Commerce, 2012, http://www.census.gov/hhes/www/poverty/about/overview/index.html.

66. Sowell, *The Vision of the Anointed*, 13.

67. Sowell, *The Economics and Politics of Race: An International Perspective* (New York: William Morrow, 1983), 125.

68. Herbert G. Gutman, *The Black Family in Slavery and Freedom, 1750–1925* (New York: Pantheon, 1976), 444.

69. Bill McAllister, "To Be Young, Male, and Black: As Group's Problems Worsen, Fatalistic Attitude Is Widespread," *Washington Post*, December 28, 1989, http://www.highbeam.com/doc/1P2-1230643.html.

70. Mary Lebreck Kelley and Virginia Macken Fitzsimons, *Understanding Cultural Diversity: Culture, Curriculum, and Community in Nursing* (Burlington, MA: Jones & Bartlett, 1999), 287.

71. Daniel Patrick Moynihan, *The Negro Family: The Case for National Action*, U.S. Department of Labor, March 1965, available online at BlackPast, http://www.blackpast.org/?q=primary/moynihan-report-1965.

72. Thomas Meehan, "Moynihan of the Moynihan Report," *New York Times*, July 31, 1966, http://www.nytimes.com/books/98/10/04/specials/moynihan-report.html?_r=2.

73. Kay S. Hymowitz, "The Black Family: 40 Years of Lies," *City Journal*, Summer 2005, http://www.city-journal.org/html/15_3_black_family.html.

74. Sam Brownback and David Blankenhorn, "End the Welfare Marriage Penalty," CitizenLink, July 8, 2010, http://www.citizenlink.com/2010/07/08/commentary-end-the-welfare-marriage-penalty/; and Rector, "Married Fathers."

75. Alex Roberts and David Blankenhorn, "The Other Marriage Penalty," Institute for American Values, Research Brief no. 3, September 2006, http://americanvalues.org/catalog/pdfs/researchbrief3.pdf.

76. Rector, "Marriage: America's Greatest Weapon Against Child Poverty"; and Steven A. Camarota, "Illegitimate Nation," Center for Immigration Studies, June 2007, http://www.cis.org/illegitimate_nation.html.

77. Stephan and Abigail Thernstrom, *America in Black and White: One Nation, Indivisible* (New York: Simon & Schuster, 1997), 240.

78. Joyce A. Martin, Brady E. Hamilton, Stephanie J. Ventura, Michelle J.K. Osterman, Sharon Kirmeyer, T.J. Mathews, and Elizabeth C. Wilson, "Births: Final Data for 2009," National Vital Statistics Reports 60, no. 1 (November 3, 2011), 8, http://www.cdc.gov/nchs/data/nvsr/nvsr60/nvsr60_01.pdf.

79. Jason L. Riley, "The State against Blacks," *Wall Street Journal*, January 22, 2011, http://online.wsj.com/article/SB10001424052748704881304576094221050061 598.html?mod=WSJ_newsreel_opinion.

80. Rector, "Married Fathers."

81. "Marriage and Poverty in the U.S.: By the Numbers," Heritage Foundation, 2010, http://thf_media.s3.amazonaws.com/2010/pdf/wm2934_bythenumbers.pdf.

82. Rector, "The Effects of Welfare Reform," Heritage Foundation, March 15, 2001, http://www.heritage.org/research/testimony/the-effects-of-welfare-reform.

83. Ibid.

84. Rector, "Married Fathers."

85. "Fatherlessness Is One of the Greatest Social Problems in Canada," Canadian Children's Rights Council, 1998, http://www.canadiancrc.com/Fatherlessness/ Fatherlessness_in_Canada.aspx; and Dick Feeman, Joseph Maiello, and Mike Jebbet, "Child Custody or Child Abuse," *Victoria Times-Colonist*, January 8, 1998.

86. Rector, "Married Fathers."

87. Sowell, "The Anti-Romney Vote," Real Clear Politics, February 9, 2012, http://www.realclearpolitics.com/articles/2012/02/09/the_anti-romney_vote_113066.html.

88. "Poverty Rate by Race/Ethnicity," Henry J. Kaiser Family Foundation, 2012, http://www.statehealthfacts.org/comparebar.jsp?ind=14&cat=1.

89. Chris Chapman et al., *Trends in High School Dropout and Completion Rates in the United States: 1972–2009*, U.S. Department of Education, October 2011, http://nces.ed.gov/pubs2012/2012006.pdf.

90. Hugh B. Price, "Hard-Fought Battle for Civil Rights Is Hardly Over," *New York Daily News*, August 29, 1994, p. 23; Bob Herbert, "Don't Flunk the Future," *New York Times*, August 13, 1998, http://www.nytimes.com/1998/08/13/opinion/in-america-don-t-flunk-the-future.html.

91. Jay P. Greene and Marcus A. Winters, "Leaving Boys Behind: Public High School Graduation Rates," Manhattan Institute for Policy Research, Civil Report no. 48, April 2006, http://www.manhattan-institute.org/html/cr_48.htm.

92. Greg Toppo, "'Crisis' Graduation Gap Found between Cities, Suburbs," *USA Today*, August 1, 2008, http://www.usatoday.com/news/education/2008-04-01-cities-suburbs-graduation_N.htm; and Blaire Briody, "School Budgets: The Worst Education Money Can Buy," *Fiscal Times*, June 6, 2011, http://www.

thefiscaltimes.com/Articles/2011/06/06/School-Budgets-The-Worst-Education-Money-Can-Buy.aspx#page1.

93. Clint Bolick, "Good Public Schools … for the Rich," Hoover Institution, October 30, 2004, No. 4, http://www.hoover.org/publications/hoover-digest/article/7057.

94. Danielle Wright, "Only 13 Percent of 2011 Black Graduates Proficient in Reading," BET News, August 23, 2011, http://www.bet.com/news/national/2011/08/23/report-only-13-percent-of-2011-black-graduates-proficient-in-reading.html.html.

95. Lydia G. Segal, *Battling Corruption in America's Public Schools* (Boston: Northeastern University Press, 2003), xix.

96. Jonah Goldberg, "Liberalism's Greatest Failure?," *The Corner* (blog), National Review Online, September 28, 2010, http://www.nationalreview.com/corner/247989/liberalisms-greatest-failure-jonah-goldberg.

97. Linda A. DiVall, "The Hollow Man," *Los Angeles Times*, August 13, 2000, http://articles.latimes.com/2000/aug/13/opinion/op-3539.

98. "Public Education Finances: 2009," U.S. Department of Commerce, U.S. Census Bureau, May 2011, http://www2.census.gov/govs/school/09f33pub.pdf.

99. "Table 262. Public Elementary and Secondary Estimated Finances: 1980 to 2009, and by State, 2009," from *Statistical Abstract of the United States: 2012*, U.S. Census Bureau, http://www.census.gov/compendia/statab/2012/tables/12s0262.pdf.

100. "How Much Money Does the United States Spend on Public Elementary and Secondary Schools?," National Center for Education Statistics, 2012, http://nces.ed.gov/fastfacts/display.asp?id=66.

101. Caroline May, "City Leaders, Think Tankers Suggest Various Causes of Detroit's High Illiteracy Rate," Daily Caller, May 10, 2011, http://dailycaller.com/2011/05/10/city-leaders-think-tankers-suggest-various-causes-of-detroits-high-illiteracy-rate/.

102. Aaron Foley, "Nation's Report Card: Detroit Students' Reading Scores Are Lowest in the Country," MLive.com, May 20, 2010, http://www.mlive.com/news/detroit/index.ssf/2010/05/nations_report_card_detroit_st.html.

103. Jonathan Oosting, "Detroit Students Notch Lowest Math Scores in History of Standardized Test," MLive.com, December 8, 2009, http://www.mlive.com/news/detroit/index.ssf/2009/12/detroit_students_notch_lowest.html.

104. "Trenton, New Jersey," City-Data.com, http://www.city-data.com/city/Trenton-New-Jersey.html.

105. Briody, "School Budgets."

106. "Camden, New Jersey," City-Data.com, http://www.city-data.com/city/Camden-New-Jersey.html.

107. Briody, "School Budgets."

108. Phillip Reese and Laurel Rosenhall, "Six-Figure Pensions Soar for California School Administrators," *Modesto Bee*, June 26, 2011, http://www.modbee.com/2011/06/26/1749157_six-figure-pensions-soar-for-california.html.

109. Kenric Ward, "Amid Cries for More Cash, $100,000+ School Salaries Soar 818 Percent," *Sunshine State News*, January 17, 2012, http://www.sunshinestatenews.com/story/amid-cries-more-cash-100000-school-salaries-soar-818-percent.

110. Reese and Rosenhall, "Six-Figure Pensions Soar for California School Administrators."

111. "Annual Secondary Education Expenditures per Student," in "10 Facts about K–12 Education Funding [Archived Information]," U.S. Department of Education, 2006, http://www2.ed.gov/about/overview/fed/10facts/edlite-chart.html; Louis Freedberg, "Federal Education Law Traps Schools in Spiral of Failure," EdSource, August 29, 2013, http://edsource.org/today/2013/federal-law-traps-schools-in-spiral-of-failure/38135#.UtNko2ByFWM; and Wilbert van der Klaauw, "Breaking the Link between Poverty and Low Student Achievement: An Evaluation of Title I," June 2005, http://www.unc.edu/~vanderkl/brlink.pdf.

112. Almena Lomax, "Mother's Day in Montgomery," originally published May 18, 1956, available online at the Martin Luther King, Jr. Research and Education Institute, http://mlk-kpp01.stanford.edu/index.php/encyclopedia/document-sentry/mothera.

113. David Horowitz, "Marc Lamont Hill's Overrated Black People List: Michael Eric Dyson," *FrontPage Magazine*, October 12, 2009, http://frontpagemag.com/2009/10/12/marc-lamont-hill's-overrated-black-people-list-michael-eric-dyson-by-david-horowitz/.

114. President John F. Kennedy, "Establishing the President's Committee on Equal Employment Opportunity," Executive Order 10925, March 6, 1961, http://www.thecre.com/fedlaw/legal6/eo10925.htm.

115. There were ritual denials that quotas were intended but since disparities in outcomes were the standard for deciding whether policies were racist the effect was the same. Herman Belz, *Equality Transformed: A Quarter-Century of Affirmative Action* (New York: Transaction, 1991), 39; Hugh Davis Graham, *The Civil Rights Era: Origins and Development of National Policy, 1960-1972* (New York: Oxford University, 1990), 111–13; and Dinesh D'Souza, *The End of Racism* (New York: Free Press, 1995), 224.

116. Stephan and Abigail Thernstrom, *America in Black and White: One Nation, Indivisible* (New York: Simon & Schuster, 1997), 172–73.

117. Ibid.

118. Ibid., 413.

119. Ibid., 414.

120. Michelle Malkin, "The Life And Death of Patrick Chavis," Philly.com, August 14, 2002, http://articles.philly.com/2002-08-14/news/25336231_1_chavis-tammaria-cotton-affirmative-action.

121. Douglas Martin, "Patrick Chavis, 50, Affirmative Action Figure," *New York Times*, August 15, 2002, http://www.nytimes.com/2002/08/15/us/patrick-chavis-50-affi rmative-action-figure.html.

122. Hilton Kramer, "Exhibit A for Quotas—Not," *New York Post*, September 2, 1997; Thomas Sowell, "An Early Quota 'Victory' Turns Out the Contrary," *New York Post*, August 28, 1997, p. 31

123. "Allan Bakke, Patrick Chavis and Affirmative Action," YouTube video, uploaded by George Roberts III, July 18, 2009, http://www.youtube.com/watch?v=shMdWYjVmCQ.

124. Robert Lerner and Althea Nagai, "Racial and Ethnic Preferences in Admissions at Five Public Medical Schools," Center for Equal Opportunity, June 14, 2001, http://www.ceousa.org/attachments/article/659/multimed.pdf; and Lerner and Nagai, "Racial and Ethnic Preferences and Consequences at the University of Maryland School of Medicine," Center for Equal Opportunity, April 3, 2001, http://www.ceousa.org/attachments/article/653/MDMED.pdf.

125. Association of American Medical Colleges, "Medical School Graduation and Attrition Rates," *Analysis in Brief* 7, no. 2 (April 2007), https://www.aamc.org/download/102346/data/.

126. Caroline Arbanas, "Age, Race, Debt Linked to Docs' Board Certification," Medical Xpress, September 22, 2011, http://medicalxpress.com/news/2011-09-age-debt-linked-docs-board.html.

127. Stephan Thernstrom, "The Scandal of the Law Schools," *Commentary*, December 1997, p. 28, http://webcache.googleusercontent.com/search?q=cache:VYqbVr-PudIJ:www.discoverthenetworks.org/Articles/The%2520Scandal%2520of%2520the%2520Law%2520Schools.docx+&cd=2&hl=en&ct=clnk&gl=us.

128. Lerner and Althea Nagai, *Racial and Ethnic Preferences at the Three Virginia Public Law Schools*, Center for Equal Opportunity, April 25, 2002, http://198.173.245.213/pdfs/VALaw.pdf.

129. Nagai, *Racial and Ethnic Preferences in Admission at the University of Arizona College of Law*, Center for Equal Opportunity, October 1, 2008, http://www.ceousa.org/attachments/article/577/AZ_Law.pdf.

130. For a comprehensive overview of the problem, see Richard Sander and Stuart Taylor Jr., *Mismatch: How Affirmative Action Hurts Students It's Intended to Help, and Why Universities Won't Admit It* (New York: Basic, 2012).

131. Ibid.

132. William G. Bowen and Derek Bok, *The Shape of the River: Long-Term Consequences of Considering Race in College and University Admissions* (Princeton: Princeton University Press, 1998), 26.

133. Scott Jaschik, "The Graduation Rate Gap," *Inside Higher Ed*, April 21, 2008, http://app3.insidehighered.com/news/2008/04/21/gradrates; and "Graduation Rate Watch – Making Minority Student Success a Priority," Kevin Carey, *American Institutes for Research*, April 18, 2008, http://www.educationsector.org/publications/graduation-rate-watch.

134. John Hawkins, "5 Common Political Beliefs That Simply Aren't True," *Townhall*, April 26, 2011, http://townhall.com/columnists/johnhawkins/2011/04/26/5_common_political_beliefs_that_simply_arent_true.

135. Thomas Sowell, "Unabated Fraud," *Washington Times*, May 26, 2003, http://www.washingtontimes.com/news/2003/may/26/20030526-104003-2403r/?page=all.

136. Adam Liptak, "For Blacks in Law School, Can Less Be More?," *New York Times*, February 13, 2005, http://www.nytimes.com/2005/02/13/weekinreview/13liptak.html?pagewanted=all.

137. Thernstrom, "The Scandal of the Law Schools."

138. Jane Yakowitz, "Marooned: An Empirical Investigation of Law School Graduates Who Fail the Bar Exam," *Journal of Legal Education* 60, no. 1 (August 2010), https://swlaw.edu/pdfs/jle/jle601yakowitz.pdf.

139. Thernstrom and Thernstrom, *America in Black and White*, 81–83.

140. Ibid.

CHAPTER 7: THE TEA PARTY AND THE GOP: CAN THIS MARRIAGE SURVIVE?

1. Alexander Eichler, "Young People More Likely to Favor Socialism Than Capitalism: Pew," Huffington Post, December 29, 2011, updated December 30, 2011, http://www.huffingtonpost.com/2011/12/29/young-people-socialism_n_1175218.html.

2. Michael Kelly, "Saint Hillary," *New York Times Magazine*, May 23, 1993 http://www.nytimes.com/1993/05/23/magazine/saint-hillary.html?src=pm&pagewanted=2.

3.   This is the phrase woven into the carpet that President Obama had installed in the Oval Office to inspire him.

4.   David Horowitz and Richard Poe, *The Shadow Party: How George Soros, Hillary Clinton, and Sixties Radicals Seized Control of the Democratic Party* (Nashville: Thomas Nelson, 2006).

CHAPTER 8: THE ART OF POLITICAL WAR

1.   Clinton launched missile strikes on these countries in the midst of the scandal to distract attention from his troubles.

2.   The Congressional Progressive Caucus is the largest membership organization in the Democratic Caucus. It now has sixty-eight members, in the 113th Congress, and is co-chaired by former Nation of Islam spokesman and left-wing extremist, Keith Ellison. "Congressional Progressive Caucus," Discover the Networks, http://www.discoverthenetworks.org/groupProfile.asp?grpid=6497.

3.   "Democratic Socialists of America," Discover the Networks, http://www.discove rthenetworks.org/groupProfile.asp?grpid=6428.

4.   Clarence Page, "The Black Caucus Teams Up with Farrakhan," *Baltimore Sun*, September 21, 1993. Shortly after making the covenant, the Black Caucus was forced to repudiate it when Farrakhan made a public statement of Jew hatred that caused a national scandal that damaged their image.

CHAPTER 9: HOW TO BEAT THE DEMOCRATS

1.   Paul Gigot, "Why Dems Let Gore Fight On and On, and … ," *Wall Street Journal*, December 1, 2000.

2.   In the wake of Florida, the political leftists who dominate America's legal faculties came out en masse to attack the Supreme Court's resolution of the crisis Gore had created. Hundreds of leftist law professors signed a tendentious public advertisement condemning the Supreme Court's ruling. An examination by legal experts Peter Berkowitz and Benjamin Wittes in the *Wilson Quarterly* shows that the alleged arguments are contrived and merely reflect the political prejudices of the signers, the vast majority of whom were not constitutional law experts. Peter Berkowitz and Benjamin Wittes, "The Professors and *Bush v. Gore*," *Wilson Quarterly*, October 29, 2001, pp. 76–89, http://www.wilsonquarterly.com/essays/

professors-and-bush-v-gore; http://www.peterberkowitz.com/theprofessorsandb ushvgore.htm.

3. Al Gore's media campaigns were run by Bob Shrum, formerly Ted Kennedy's press secretary. Shrum had previously distinguished himself with a TV ad against the California anti-discrimination initiative (Proposition 209), which featured hooded Ku Klux Klan members burning crosses. The voice-over in Shrum's ad, which was spoken by actress Candace Bergen, linked Newt Gingrich, Ward Connerly, California governor Pete Wilson, and former Ku Klux Klan grand dragon David Duke as supporters of the measure, which the ad claimed would deprive blacks and women of their rights. The proposition Shrum was attacking read as follows: "The state shall not discriminate against, or grant preferential treatment to, any individual or group on the basis of race, sex, color, ethnicity, or national origin in the operation of public employment, public education, or public contracting." In his ad, Shrum ignored the clear meaning of the text. He used a similar ad to defeat Ellen Sauerbrey in a gubernatorial campaign in Maryland in 1998. The ad, falsely painting her as a racist, was so outrageous that Baltimore's African American mayor Kurt Schmoke, a Democrat, publicly dissociated himself from it. To Al Gore, on the other hand, Shrum's low character and ruthless tactics were reasons to hire him for a presidential run.

4. The prediction was made in July. Alan Bernstein, "Political Forecasters Sticking with Gore Despite All the Polls," *Houston Chronicle*, November 2, 2000, p. 13A, http://www.academia.edu/2824849/.

5. "Antonio Gramsci," Discover the Networks, http://www.discoverthenetworks. org/individualProfile.asp?indid=2390.

6. Kevin Sack, "The 2000 Campaign: The Vice President; With Broad Themes, Rivals Seek to Energize Voters," *New York Times*, November 5, 2000, pp. A1, A32, http://www.nytimes.com/2000/11/05/us/2000-campaign-vice-president-with-broad-themes-rivals-seek-energize-voters.html.

7. The phrase "three-fifths of a human being" refers to slaves, not to black persons, many of whom were freemen. The so-called three-fifths compromise was proposed by anti-slavery Framers in order to diminish the electoral power of the slave-holding South. Under the compromise, slaves were to be counted as three-fifths of a person for the purpose of apportioning congressional representation.

8. Rich Lowry and Ramesh Ponnuru, "Bush's Better Inclination," *New York Times*, October 25, 2000, http://www.nytimes.com/2000/10/25/opinion/bush-s-better-inclination.html.

9.   This quotation is often attributed to Tytler, but its source is in fact unknown. Its popularity is a measure of its prescience, which does not depend on the identity of its author.

10. "Transcript of George W. Bush's Acceptance Speech," transcript of speech at the Republican National Convention, August 3, 2000, available online at ABC News, http://abcnews.go.com/Politics/story?id=123214&page=4.

11. The exception was Jimmy Carter, a military man and a Southerner.

12. *Hardball With Chris Matthews*, MSNBC, November 27, 2000.

13. As president, Clinton himself attended meetings of the Second Socialist International. I recently heard Henry Kissinger characterize these visits as inappropriate for an American president, since he attends them not as a party official, but as a head of state.

14. Cleta Mitchell, "How Democrats Wage Political War," *Wall Street Journal*, November 20, 2000, http://online.wsj.com/news/articles/SB122574984794694617.

15. Michael Kelly, "Saint Hillary," *New York Times Sunday Magazine*, May 23, 1993, http://www.nytimes.com/1993/05/23/magazine/saint-hillary.html?pagewanted=all&src=pm.

16. "Propaganda and Public Relations Work in the United States," chapter 5 in Paul Seabury and Walter A. McDougall, eds., *The Grenada Papers* (San Francisco: Institute for Contemporary Studies, 1984). An illustrative case is the selection of Carlottia Scott as the political issues director of the Democrat National Committee in May 1999. Scott is the former mistress of the Marxist dictator of Grenada, and the former chief of staff for retired Congressman Ron Dellums (D-Berkeley), a radical whom Democrats made the head of the House Subcommittee on Military Installations with top security clearance. Every year during the Cold War, Dellums submitted his own military budget to Congress proposing to cut U.S. Defense spending by 75 percent. When the Marines liberated Grenada, in 1983, they discovered a cache of Scott's love letters to the former dictator. In one of them she wrote: "Ron [Dellums] has become truly committed to Grenada.... He's really hooked on you and Grenada and doesn't want anything to happen to building the Revolution and making it strong. He really admires you as a person and even more so as a leader ... The only other person that I know of that he expresses such admiration for is Fidel." When Congressman Dellums retired, in 1998, Bill Clinton's Secretary of Defense William Cohen awarded him the highest civilian medal the Pentagon can bestow.

17. As was later revealed, Shepard's death was drug-related and had nothing to do with his being gay. Stephen Jimenez, *The Book of Matt: Hidden Truths about the Murder of Matthew Shepard* (Hanover, NH: Steerforth, 2013).

18. "Equal Time with Paul Begala and Oliver North," MSNBC, Nov 13, 2000, http://www.angelfire.com/hi5/pearly/htmls/begala-banana.html.

19. Ronald Taylor killed three people in Pittsburgh, and Colin Ferguson went on a shooting spree against whites and Asians on a Long Island commuter train. Tom Barnes, "Ronald Taylor Gets Death Sentence," *Post-Gazette*, November 12, 2001, http://old.post-gazette.com/regionstate/20011112taylorreg2p2.asp; and James Barron, "Death on the L.I.R.R.," *New York Times*, December 9, 1993, http://www.nytimes.com/1993/12/09/nyregion/death-lirr-overview-portrait-suspect-emerges-shooting-li-train.html?pagewanted=all&src=pm.

20. Cited in Dick Morris, *Behind the Oval Office: Winning the Presidency in the Nineties* (New York: Random House, 1997), 268.

21. George Stephanopoulos, *All Too Human: A Political Education* (New York: Little, Brown, 1999).

22. Congressman Patrick Kennedy told Democrats in Pennsylvania, "All you need to do is look at Newt Gingrich, Trent Lott, Dick Armey, Tom DeLay ... There's always been a fascist crowd in every society." Jeff Jacoby, "Slander Is Just Fine When the Left Does It," *Boston Globe*, December 28, 2000, p. A15, http://pqasb.pqarchiver.com/boston/doc/405367199.html?FMT=ABS&FMTS=ABS:FT&type=current&date=Dec+28%2C+2000&author=Jacoby%2C+Jeff&pub=Boston+Globe&edition=&startpage=&desc=SLANDER+IS+JUST+FINE+WHEN+THE+LEFT+DOES+IT.

23. "The VNS exit poll showed Gore winning majorities of the vote on all the issues he emphasized as part of his populist approach; indeed, among voters who said issues, rather than 'qualities,' mattered most, Gore ran up a healthy lead of 55% to 40%." Ruy Teixeira, "Lessons for Next Time," *American Prospect*, December 19, 2001, http://prospect.org/article/lessons-next-time.

24. Peter Roff, "The Truth about Barack Obama, Mitt Romney, and Welfare Reform," *U.S. News & World Report*, September 24, 2012, http://www.usnews.com/opinion/blogs/peter-roff/2012/09/24/the-truth-about-barack-obama-mitt-romney-and-welfare-reform.

25. An accomplishment largely undone by the Obama administration. Robert Rector, "Obama Guts Welfare Reform," Heritage Foundation, September 12, 2012, http://www.heritage.org/issues/welfare/welfare-reform.

26. Louis Sahagun, "50% of Pupils Not Ready to Pass, L.A. District Says," *Los Angeles Times*, December 1, 1999, http://articles.latimes.com/1999/dec/01/news/mn-39443.

INDEX

1 percent, the, 2, 65, 80, 90

9/11 attacks, 24, 26, 32, 35, 37

A

Abedin, Huma, 31–32

Abu Ghraib prison, 36

Affirmative Action, 98–104

Affordable Care Act, 5, 46. *See also* Obamacare

African Americans, 5, 12, 17–20, 59, 61–63, 66, 82, 86–91, 93, 95, 98–104, 126, 142, 145, 149, 155, 164. *See also* black Americans

African National Congress, 42

Alinsky, Saul, 45–46, 72

al Qaeda, 25–28, 33, 49–50, 54

al-Qaradawi, Yusuf, 27

America, Americans
    constitutional rights of, 42–43
    and individual freedom, 10, 21, 56, 74–77, 81, 129
    middle class of, 18, 66, 103, 151

    national debt of, xiii, 1, 76
    as a pluralistic society, 55, 118, 124
    as race conscious and prejudiced, 58
    social contract of, 41, 43

American Dream Downpayment Initiative, 87

Americans for Prosperity, 30

Americans for Prosperity super PAC, 30

Art of Political War, The, 117–37, 143

Asian Americans, 3, 12, 84, 90, 100, 155

Association of Community Organization for Reform Now (ACORN), 83, 85

Axelrod, David, 39

Ayers, William, 46

B

Bachmann, Michele, 31–32

Bakke, Allan, 99–100

Battling Corruption in America's Public Schools, 96

Becker, Gary, 84

Benghazi, 26, 49

Berlin Wall, 147

betrayal, xiii, 30, 33, 65, 112
    Democrats' betrayal during Iraq
        War, 33–37, 50–53

Beyoncé, 49

big government, 79, 89, 95–98, 150, 153

bin Laden, Osama, 25, 29, 32

black Americans, 12, 17–20, 57, 59, 62, 66,
    75, 81–93, 95–105, 114, 126–27, 132,
    143, 162. *See also* African Americans

black underclass, 89–95, 104
    War on Poverty's creation of,
        91–103

Boehner, John, 32, 111, 113

Bok, Derek, 101

Bolsheviks, 44, 71

Bork, Robert, 142

Bowen, William, 101

Boxer, Barbara, 125

Bush, George W., 23–24, 30–33, 35–36,
    50–54, 87–88, 139, 142–43, 145, 149,
    151, 164

C

Caddell, Patrick, 152

campaign narrative, 12–16, 58

Carson, Ben, xiii

Carter, Jimmy, 18, 23, 30, 59, 83, 152

Cavanaugh, James, 60

Center for Responsible Lending, 87

Chavis, Patrick, 100

Chicago strike, the, 19

Christian Right, the, 132

Christians, 50, 70, 126, 132

Christie, Chris, 13, 19–20

"citizens of the world," 48, 50

civil rights, 39, 83–84, 98–99, 103, 149,
    153, 156

class warfare rhetoric, 2–4

Clinton, Bill, 7, 18, 35, 50, 52, 59, 79–80,
    88, 117–20, 122, 126–27, 136–37,
    145, 153, 155–57, 160, 162
    administration of, xii, 79, 83–85,
        132
    budget negotiations of 1998,
        136–37
    impeachment of, 117–20
    "New Democrat" strategy of, 153
    response to Lewinsky scandals,
        119–20, 156–57

Clinton, Hillary, 7, 27–28, 31, 49, 110,
    127, 154
    response to Benghazi, 49

CNN, 4

Cold War, 23–24, 41, 44, 50, 76–77, 109,
    129, 146–48, 152

communism, 40, 42, 44–45, 76, 109, 129,
    153

Communist Party, 39–40, 45, 60

Communist progressive Left, 40

Community Reinvestment Act (CRA),
    18, 82

compassion, 80–81, 127, 135, 142, 145,
    149, 160
    as a winning virtue, 151–52

compromise, 73–74, 109, 111
    as necessary to democracy, 74

Congressional Black Caucus, 132

Congressional Progressive Caucus, 89,
    132

Congress of Racial Equality, 98

conservative, conservatism, xi–xiv, 34, 48,
     56–61, 65–67, 81, 121, 125, 132, 145,
     142, 151–52, 154, 163
     "compassionate conservatism,"
          135–38, 142, 149, 151–52
     demonization of, 9–10, 45, 56, 59,
          72, 80, 155
     different types of, 30–31, 70, 73,
          76, 107–13, 148
     fatalism of, xii
     grassroots, 41, 72–73, 107–8
     pessimism of, xi, 147–48
     unifying cause of, 74–77
     values of, 41–44, 48, 52, 74–76,
          111, 118–20, 129, 151
     view of politics of, 7–8, 11–12,
          41, 43, 48, 52, 54, 70, 72–75,
          110–12, 123

Constitution of South Africa, 42

Constitution, U.S., 40, 41–43, 48, 54, 56,
     74–75, 112, 117–18, 122, 140, 145,
     148–49

contraception, 9

Corzine, Jon, 59

Crossroads super PAC, 30

Cruz, Ted, 107–8, 112
     filibuster against funding
          Obamacare, 108, 112
     as a worthy conservative leader,
          107–8

Cuomo, Mario, 15, 17, 152

D

Dean, Howard, 51–52

Democratic convention 2012, 13–15

Democrats, Democratic Party

acting in unity and solidarity, 64,
     69–71, 73
campaign themes of, 1
emotional hate campaign of, 11
how to beat the, 139–63
Leftist infiltration of, 46, 55, 113
missionary mentality of, 111
as relying on bribery and fear,
     150–51
signature programs of, xi
as social missionaries, social
     redeemers, 7–9, 44, 70, 71,
     110–12, 153
social schemes of, xii, 8, 10, 45, 47,
     60, 74–75, 102, 109, 140, 150,
     162
superior political strategy of, xi,
     2, 15–16, 46, 59, 121, 129, 136,
     147, 157
unifying idea of, 70

Department of Housing and Urban
     Development (HUD), 85–86

Detroit, 17–18, 58, 60–62, 95–97, 114
     as example of Democrat control,
          17, 60–62, 114

discrimination, 42, 82–83, 85, 90–91, 99,
     103, 149

dishonesty, xiii, 12, 45–46
     as part of the progressive cause,
          45–46

Dodd, Christopher, 86

Dole, Bob, 7, 145, 155

E

economic crisis of 2008, 81

economic redistribution, 76

education. *See* private education; public
    education
Education Savings Bill, 131
Edwards, John, 35, 51
Egypt, 26–29, 31, 37, 41–42, 57. *See also*
    Muslim Brotherhood.
elections, xi, xiii, 1–5, 11, 15, 23–24, 56, 58,
    66, 73, 80, 109, 128, 133, 139–42, 146,
    153, 156–58
    "caring" as the central issue during,
        2, 152
    consequences of, 56
Emanuel, Rahm, 59
Equal Employment Opportunity Com-
    mission, 99
equality, 8–9, 43, 58, 71, 74–75, 90, 98–99,
    104
Espionage Act, 36
Esposito, John, 32

F

fairness, 20, 58, 65, 76, 124, 157
Fallujah, 36
Fannie Mae, 86
Farrakhan, Louis, 132
fear, 3–5, 11–13, 32, 36, 45, 72, 119, 123,
    125–27, 129, 143–46, 150–51, 158
    as a political weapon, 3–5, 11–13,
        123, 125–27, 144–46
Federal Reserve Bank of Boston, 83–84
Federal Reserve Board, 84
Fenty, Adrian, 62–64
fiscal restraint, 23
Fluke, Sandra, 9, 65
food stamps, 17, 59, 61, 65, 92–93

foreclosure rates, 87–88
Fort Hood massacre, 25
Founding Fathers, Founders, 41–44,
    74–76, 119, 140–41, 151
Frank, Barney, 86, 88, 127, 133
Freddie Mac, 86
freedom, 10, 21, 28, 41, 43–44, 47, 56,
    74–77, 81, 129, 158
    individual freedom, 10, 21, 56,
        74–77, 81, 129
French Revolution, 56

G

Gaddafi, Muammar, 26–27
Gaza, 29
Ginsburg, Justice Ruth Bader, 41–42, 48
"Global War on Terror," 25
Gore, Al, 33, 35–36, 51, 96, 144, 146–49,
    151, 154, 159, 162
government control, 21, 47
government shutdown, 40, 107–8
grassroots movements, 41, 70, 73, 83,
    112–13
Greenlining Institute, 85
"Green Revolution," 25
gutter tactics, 142

H

Hamas, 27, 49–50
hate crimes, 142, 145, 158
Hezbollah, 49
Hill, Anita, 156
Hispanic, Hispanics, 5, 17–20, 62, 65–66,
    81–89, 93, 95–99, 101, 105, 114, 133–
    35, 143, 162

Hitler, Adolf, 29

Home Mortgage Disclosure Act, 86

homeowners, home ownership, 81–95

House Banking Committee, 82

House Committee on Financial Services, 86

Housing and Community Development Act of 1977, 82

housing market
collapse of the, 18, 81, 82

Humphrey, Hubert, 6

Hussain, Rashad, 32

Hussein, Saddam, 35, 37, 51–53
regime of, 34

I

illiteracy rates, 19, 61, 63, 162

improvised explosive devices, 25

inner cities, 17–19, 60, 62, 64, 66, 94–96, 104, 143–44, 160, 162

inner-city schools, 19, 62, 64, 95–96, 137, 162

Iran, 1, 24–30, 33–34, 37–38, 49, 53, 77

Iran hostage crisis, 30

Iraq, 1, 25–26, 30–31, 33–37, 50–54, 122

Iraq Liberation Act, 35, 50

Iraq War, 25–26, 31, 33–37, 50–54

"Iraq War Syndrome," 37
media campaign against Iraq War, 36

Islam, 24–29, 31–32, 34–36, 38, 50, 53, 77

"Islamophobe," 32

J

Jarrett, Valerie, 39

Jay-Z, 49

Jews, 27–29, 50, 70, 90
extermination of, 27–29, 50

jihadists, 25–27, 31, 33–34, 37, 53

job creators, 5, 16–17, 56

job destroyers, 16–17, 57

Johnson, Eddie Bernice, 89

Johnson, Lyndon, xi, 23, 91–92, 99, 148

K

Kennedy, John F., 6, 23, 98, 113, 127, 152–53

Kennedy, Ted, 33, 100, 137, 152

Kerry, John, 7, 28, 35–36, 51–52

Kilpatrick, Kwame, 61

King, Martin Luther, 90, 98, 103

Kosygin, Alexei, 49

L

Lebanon, 37

Lehane, Chris, ix

Lenin, 44

Lewinsky, Monica, 119–20, 156
Republican reaction to, 119–20
scandal, 118–20

liberals, 39–40, 42, 46, 57, 60, 80, 109–10, 117, 122, 126–27, 132–33, 137, 147, 157

Libya, 26–28, 30, 53–54

"living constitution," 41

loans, 18, 82–88

Ludwig, Eugene, 85

lying, 6, 9, 52–53
as spin in politics, 6

M

Madison, James, 42, 75

Mali, 27, 37

Martinez, Susana, 13

Marxism, Marxist, 55, 154, 158

Marx, Karl, 56

McAuliffe, Terry, 59

McCain, John, 32, 37, 57, 113

McCarthyism, "McCarthyite," 32, 120–21, 127

McGovern, George, 7, 82, 113, 152

medical savings accounts, 47

medical school acceptance rates, 99–100

Medicare, xi, 8, 48, 74, 109, 156

minorities, 1, 3, 10, 11, 14–15, 17–21, 23, 28, 58–62, 64–67, 71, 76, 81–89, 94–96, 101–2, 104–5, 110, 111, 113–14, 126, 129, 132, 135, 137–38, 142, 145, 158–59, 161, 163–64

Mitchell, Cleta, 153

Morial, Marc, 189

Morris, Dick, 7, 155, 160

mortgages, 18, 82–84, 86–89

Moynihan, Daniel Patrick, 92–93

Mubarak, Hosni, 27

Muslim Brotherhood, 1, 27–32, 41, 49–50, 57, 77

Obama's support of, 27–30, 32, 41, 50, 57

N

NAACP, 98–99, 142

Naseef, Abdullah Omar, 32

National Review, 149

national security, 23–24, 28–38

National Urban League, 89, 98

New Deal, 79, 152

New York Times, 36, 86

Nixon, Richard, 145

nuclear weapons, 24–25, 29, 35, 38, 52–53

O

Obama, Barack

2008 campaign and, 11–12, 36–37

2012 campaign and, 2–5, 13, 15–16, 19, 30, 33–34, 37, 44, 65, 79, 113

as an absentee executive, 57

campaign promises of, 3, 5, 7, 11–12, 47, 57

economy under, 17, 56, 59, 65–66, 79

foreign policy under, 24–34, 37–38, 41, 53–54

housing crisis and, 18, 83, 88–89

ideology of, 39–50, 56, 70, 72, 107–8, 110

as a liar, 57–58, 113

private education and, 67

Obamacare. See also "Patient Protection and Affordable Care Act"

costs of, 47, 65–66, 76

opposition to, 58, 65, 70, 74, 108–9

passage of, 7–8

as socialist program, xii, 8, 46–48, 69

website, xiii

Occupy Wall Street, 65, 69, 80

original innocence, 43

out-of-wedlock birthrates, 90, 92–93

P

Palestine, 37

"Patient Protection and Affordable Care Act," 46. See also Obamacare

patriotism, 48

Pelosi, Nancy, 14, 59

political strategy, 147

    Democratic, xi, 2, 15–16, 46, 59–60, 121, 129, 136, 147–49, 153

    Republican, xi–xiv, 58, 64, 118, 125, 149, 152, 164

    successful, 64, 127, 133, 157

political war

    principles of, 119, 121–38

politicians,

    demagogic, 64

    hope and, 146

    manipulation by, 94, 127, 129, 144

progressive, 9, 81–89, 94

politics

    art of, xiii, 144

    class warfare and, 3–4, 131

    Democratic view of, xi–xii, 4, 6–8, 44, 69, 72, 74, 110–11 113–14, 122, 132, 139–41, 153–54, 163–65

    as divisive, 3–5

    emotions in, 1, 3–4, 12–13, 123, 125–28, 143–45

    image in, 125–31, 144, 155, 159–60

    Republican view of, xi, 5–6, 67, 109, 122, 140, 158

    the side of the people in, 117–19, 123, 138, 157

    style in, 3–4, 115

    tactical principles of, 6–7, 11–12, 109

    versus policy, 108, 122, 141–43, 159

    as war, xiii, 17, 44, 72, 110, 112, 123–25, 139, 141, 143–44, 146

presidential campaign of 1972, 7, 113, 152

presidential election of 2000, 23, 139–42, 147–64

presidential election of 2012, 2–5, 11–15, 18–19, 24–34, 37, 56, 62, 65, 80, 112

principle of non-intervention, 26

private education, 19, 63, 66, 96, 99, 131–32, 137

progressives

    beliefs of, xii, 7–11, 41–54, 57–58, 70–76, 79–81, 105, 110–11, 157

    contempt for American past, 41–43, 140, 153

    as defenders of poor, 58

    as disguised Communists, 39–40

    electoral power of, 56

    harm done to the poor by, 60–61, 64–67, 81–105, 114, 137–38, 162

    hatred of conservatives, 9–10, 72, 80

public education

    bureaucrats, 20, 97, 104, 131–32

    George W. Bush and, 142, 151

    minority victims of, 19, 61, 76, 87–88, 90, 95–96, 104, 137–38, 162–63

    money spent on, 63, 66–67, 98, 131–32, 136

    unions and, 63–65, 104, 136–37

    vouchers and, 20, 66

    in Washington, D.C., 63–65

R

racial preferences, 98, 101–4, 163. See also affirmative action

racism, racists, 41, 93, 150, 153, 46, 48, 154, 158
  Democrats and, 93, 114, 132, 160–61
  mortgage industry and, 82–84, 82–85, 87
  Republicans accused of, 9, 58–59, 109, 124, 126–27, 133, 135, 142, 149, 151, 154–56, 163

Reagan, Ronald, 6, 23, 30, 138, 145–47, 152, 157

Regents of the University of California V. Bakke (1977), 99–100

Reid, Harry, 40, 108

Renaissance Weekends, xii

Reno, Janet, 84–85

Republican Party, Republicans
  2000 election and, 140, 147–57
  administrative approach to election campaigns, 5
  approach to the welfare system, 159–62
  business mentality of, 111, 135–36, 140, 158, 160
  campaign narrative of the, 12–14, 159
  Clinton and impeachment, 119–22
  demonization of the, 6–11, 13–15, 57–58, 65–66, 71–72, 80, 109, 126–27, 130, 132, 144–45, 149, 151, 154–56, 158–59
  differences with Democrats, 6–11, 13–15, 17, 21, 35–37, 40, 48, 69–70, 109–10, 114, 123–24, 129, 132, 156, 158
  disunity of, 70, 73, 108
  diversity among, 24, 69–70, 128–29, 164

  electoral losses of the, 1–2, 4–5, 16, 21
  establishment of the, 30, 111–13, 151
  "Gold Star" Republicans, 142, 144, 158
  national convention 2012, 13–14, 19–20, 29
  national security and, 23–38, 53, 76–77
  pessimism of, xi–xiii
  political strategy of, xi, 1–6, 11, 16–18, 24–28, 30–31, 57–58, 62, 118, 125, 127, 135–37
  respect for the people, 117–18, 138, 145
  as a rural party, 163–64
  and the Tea Party, 73, 107–14
  unifying idea of the, 76–77, 129, 148
  values of the, 3, 129–30, 140–41, 151, 164
  winning strategy for, xi, 17–19, 21, 38, 64, 66, 118, 130–33, 138, 145, 152, 157–64

Restoration Weekend, xi–xiii

Reuss, Henry, 82–83

Rhee, Michelle, 63–64

Rice, Condoleezza, 13

"Roadmap for America's Future," 11–12

Romney, Ann, 13

Romney, Mitt
  47 percent comment of, xi
  defeat by Barack Obama, 2–5, 9, 12, 15–17
  election strategy of, 11–12, 16, 26, 30, 56–57, 65, 113
  foreign policy and, 29–31, 33–34, 37

Rousseau, Jean-Jacques, 43

Rove, Karl, 30, 108

Rubio, Marco, 13

Rules for Radicals, 45–46, 72

Ryan, Paul, 11–12, 65

S

school vouchers, 20, 66, 96, 163

Sebelius, Kathleen, 58

Segal, Lydia G., 96

sexism, 41, 153–53

"Shadow Party, the," 110

Shape of the River, The, 101

single-parent households, 61, 90, 93–94

sixties, the, 46, 55, 92

Smiley, Tavis, 59

socialism, socialists
    disguised as liberals, 40–41, 46, 56,
        59, 71, 132–33, 148, 153
    entitlements and, 42, 47, 109
    failures of, xii, 8, 48, 79–80, 109–10,
        150
    revolution, 39
    unrealistic expectations of, 39, 43,
        59, 109–11

socialized medicine, 48

social justice, 42, 76
    progressives and, xii, 7–8, 21, 39,
        43, 71, 74, 82–83, 88, 109–11, 114

Social Security, xi, 8, 48, 74, 109, 142, 151

Somalia, 37

Soros, George, 56, 59, 110

sound bites, 4, 11, 127–31, 136, 141

Soviet Russia, Soviet Union, 23, 42, 45, 49,
    146–48

Sowell, Thomas, 88, 94, 102

Steele, Shelby, 98

Stephanopoulos, George, 155

Stevens, Christopher, 49

Syria, 26–30, 33, 37, 49, 53, 57, 69, 77

T

Take No Prisoners Campaigns, xiv

tax cuts, 13, 56, 152

taxes
    economic effects of, 13, 60, 158
    increases in, 6, 14, 60, 65, 146, 148
    Obamacare and, 56
    political messaging and, 6, 13–14,
        128, 130–31, 135–39, 150,
        158–60

teacher unions, 19–20, 62, 136, 96, 137,
    163

Tea Party, 107–14
    differences with Republican
        establishment, 107, 111–13
    fights with Republican
        establishment, 108, 112

Tehran, 33

Tenet, George, 52

terrorists, terrorism, 24–27, 35–37, 46,
    49–50, 53, 155

Thomas, Clarence, 126, 142, 156–57

Thompson, Robert, 62

tort reform, 47

Trotsky, Leon, 71

Truman, Harry, 23, 152

truth in labeling, 130–33

"two Americas," 79–80

Tytler, Alexander, 150, 153

U

underdog, 16, 58
    as the key to American politics,
        12–14, 121, 129, 134–35, 138,
        157–61
United Nations, 26, 35, 50–51, 54
unity, 70–71, 134, 148

V

Vietnam War, 6–7
voters
    in 2000 election, 51
    in 2012 election, 1, 4–6
    Democratic tactics with, 1–2,
        4–5, 11–12, 15–16, 23, 80, 94,
        112–13, 123, 141–45, 150
    fraud and, 9
    low-information, xiii
    political priorities of, xiii, 2, 127,
        130, 135, 144–46, 150, 154,
        157–58
    Republican communications with,
        3–4, 10–13, 23, 112–13, 131–32,
        141–42, 151

W

war on freedom, 76
"War on Poverty," xi, 91, 103, 109
Washington, D.C., 61–65, 67, 95–96, 129,
    160
Washington, George, 157
Washington Post, 32, 36
Watergate, 23, 118, 140
weapons of mass destruction, 35, 51–52
welfare
    damage to families by, 30–31, 74,
        91, 93–94, 104
    Detroit and, 114
    growth of programs, 23, 91, 131,
        153, 159–60
    ineffectiveness of, 91, 103–4, 153
    reform of, 118, 126, 160–62
    Republicans and, 81, 131, 145,
        159–61
women, 53, 75, 156
    Democrats as party of, 5, 9, 17, 58,
        65, 129, 135, 158
    Islamic countries and, 28
    marriage rates of, 92–93
    war on, 1, 9–11, 14–15, 17, 58, 65,
        71–72, 109–10, 113, 154
Wong, Alex, 26
Wright, Jeremiah, 46

Y

Yemen, 37
Young, Coleman, 60–61